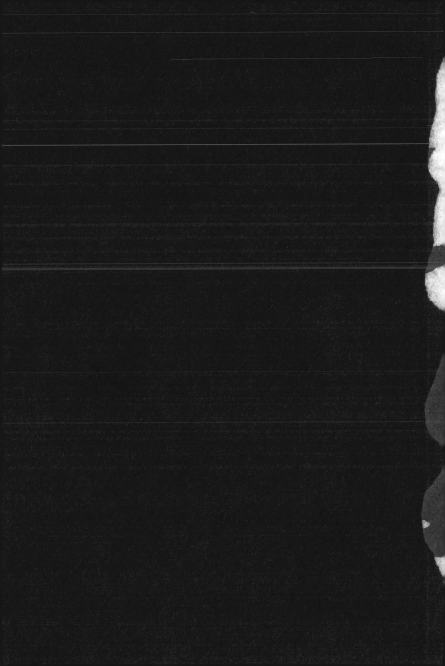

The New York Book of Dance

THE NEW YORK BOOK OF DANCE

TERRY TRUCCO

WITH ILLUSTRATIONS BY EMILY LISKER

CITY & COMPANY · NEW YORK

City & Company
22 West 23rd Street
New York, N.Y. 10010

Printed in the United States of America
Design by Leah Lococo

Library of Congress Cataloging-in-Publication Data
is available upon request.

ISBN 1-885492-22-7
First Edition

PUBLISHER'S NOTE: Neither City & Company nor the author
has any interest, financial or personal, in the venues listed in this book. No
fees were paid or services rendered in exchange for inclusion in these pages.
Please also note that every effort was made to ensure that information
regarding addresses, phone numbers, and prices was accurate
and up-to-date at the time of publication.

The New York Book of Dance

Contents

INTRODUCTION   **9**

Dance in New York City

CHAPTER ONE   **13**

Bright Lights, Big Stages

Theaters, studios, and performance spaces
that frequently host dance.

CHAPTER TWO   **23**

Home Town Troupes and Performers . . . and Slightly Beyond

Top New York-based companies and performers specializing
in ballet, modern and contemporary dance, ballroom dance, jazz, tap,
and hip-hop, ethnic dance, folk dance, and dancing on skates.
Noteworthy companies in New Jersey and Connecticut.

CHAPTER THREE   **93**

Dance It Yourself: Where to Take Lessons

Where to study ballet, modern and contemporary
dance, jazz, hip-hop, and tap, ballroom dance, ethnic dance,
skate dancing, therapeutic dance; the megastudios.

CHAPTER FOUR   **129**

Dance Kids New York

Classes, camps, and scholarships.

CHAPTER FIVE   143

Dance Academics

Where to take courses—and get a degree—in dance history,
movement theory, notation, and related disciplines.
In New York, Westchester, Long Island, Connecticut, and New Jersey.

CHAPTER SIX   151

Gotta Dance

Places to go dancing: Ballroom and Latin, swing, classic ballroom, tap,
hip-hop, house, and theme dancing, folk and country, and skate dancing.

CHAPTER SEVEN   163

Being the Best: Competitive Dance

Competitions in ballroom, Latin, and ballet.

CHAPTER EIGHT   167

Dance Gear and Memorabilia

CHAPTER NINE   175

Bargains

Freebies, $12 and under, and discount tickets.

A FINAL WORD   179

Going Backstage

INDEX   181

Dance in New York City

MY LOVE OF DANCE dates from my first day in the Baby Class, at age three-and-a-half, when I was taught the five basic positions and told to skip across the room. The combination of pure movement and Miss Betty's Chanel No. 5 was infectious. By the time I had reached my teens, I'd been to *The Nutcracker* in nearby San Francisco, had watched countless old Fred and Ginger movies, and was a seasoned recital veteran, with a closet full of pink tutus. West Coast dance was fine, but I knew there was something more, a place where seeing a performance didn't have to be an Event.

New York, where I moved in my twenties, was a revelation. There seemed to be a dance studio on almost every block, offering classes I'd never dreamed existed. The instructors had performed with New York City Ballet or Martha Graham or in a Bob Fosse musical on Broadway. The dingy upstairs classrooms, with their grand pianos, mirrored walls and chipping pink paint, seemed hopelessly atmospheric—part *Red Shoes*, part *A Chorus Line*.

And for the hearty, there was a performance *somewhere* nearly every night. The biggest problem was choosing. The Joffrey or the Limón Company? Paul Taylor or the Jerome Robbins review on Broadway? Not everything was terrific, but somehow it was less excruciating to sit through an unsuccessful dance performance than a bad play.

I realized just how unique New York was when I moved overseas for eight years. Tokyo and London, where I lived, are not exactly backwater towns, unless you're a dance enthusiast. I saw some superb butoh and contemporary dance in Japan and watched London's Royal Ballet pull itself out of its mid-1980s doldrums. But the memorable performances always seemed to be by visiting American troupes, usually from New York. The dance lover in me cheered when, five years ago, I came home.

As a quick historic overview shows, New York's position as the nation's, and arguably the world's, premiere dance city is no mystery. New York's status as a ballet capital took shape when Lincoln Kirstein met George Balanchine in London in 1933 and shared his dream of starting a company of homegrown American dancers with its own school. By the time New York City Ballet made its official debut in 1948, New York was also home to Ballet Theater, Lucia Chase's hugely popular troupe of international stars.

New York also became mecca for the moderns, from Martha Graham, who established her company and school here in the 1920s, to Merce Cunningham, who set up shop in the early 1950s. Broadway, with its insatiable appetite for musicals, high kicks, and leggy chorus girls, made New York an incubator for theatrical jazz dance, long before Bugsy Siegel dreamed up Las Vegas. And uptown clubs and theaters, like the Savoy and the Apollo, dispatched infusions of inventive vernacular dances, such as the Lindy hop, to the rest of the world. New York even became a center for folk dance as scores of immigrants poured in.

These days, as regional companies flourish in everything from ballet to Afro-Caribbean, New York is no longer the nation's only dancing town, but it is still the biggest and the best. The selection of topflight classes remains unparalleled, and when studios and universities seek out guest instructors, they usually place phone calls to area codes 212 or 718. Despite the throat-choking cost of theater rentals, rehearsal space, and tickets, New York is still *the* place to perform. And Manhattan, that shopper's paradise, is the place to effortlessly pick up a pair of ballroom shoes or a flamenco skirt.

In fact, there's so much dance in New York, it's easy to become overwhelmed. This book attempts to bring a bit of order to the dance world, offering a sample of the city's performance companies, classes, backstage tours, shopping possibilities, bargain tickets, and places to kick up your heels and go dancing. It's not comprehensive—you'd need a volume the size of the Yellow Pages for that. But it's a start and, one hopes, a hint of the irresistible pleasures that await dance aficionados in New York.

CHAPTER ONE

Bright Lights, Big Stages

AS BEFITS A DANCE and performance capital, New York City has no shortage of stages. One can almost always find a dance performance *somewhere*, whether on the lofty, velvet-draped stage of the Metropolitan Opera House or in the bustling lobby of Grand Central Station. Ballet companies, big by definition, gravitate to enormous houses like New York State Theater and City Center. But dancers can dance almost anywhere, as long as the floor has bounce (no shin-splinting concrete, please) and there's room for an audience.

As rents have risen and grants have dried up, cost-conscious dancers have abandoned conventional theaters and gone to unexpected spaces, from tiny studios with cushions tossed on the floor to libraries and even lawns. Downtown Manhattan, in particular, is a maze of miniature spaces surprisingly sympathetic to dance.

The following is a sampling of the city's busiest dance halls, from vast performance palaces to the snuggest studios. Some, like Dance Theater Workshop's Bessie Shönberg Theater, produce seasons, offering subscribers an effortless, and often money-saving, way to see a cross–section of companies. Rental spaces, in contrast, rarely have mailing or subscription lists. Still, they, too, merit a quick call to the box office if you're in the mood for dancing.

∼ GRAND SCALE ∼

BROOKLYN ACADEMY OF MUSIC (BAM)
30 Lafayette Ave., Brooklyn; (718) 636-4111
Opened in 1859, the Brooklyn Academy of Music is America's oldest performing arts center. But the classic, 2,000-seat opera house you see today actually dates from 1908, after a fire destroyed the original structure. Martha Graham, Anna Sokolow, and the Ballet Russe de Monte Carlo appeared here in years past, and since 1967, when the building was saved from razing, dance has figured big in BAM's annual presentations, from ballet (Dance Theater of Harlem, Pennsylvania Ballet) to experimental (Pina Bausch) to in-between (Mark Morris's *The Hard Nut*). There's a mailing list and subscription list for dance. Big event: the annual fall Next Wave festival of contemporary artists.

BROOKLYN CENTER FOR THE PERFORMING ARTS AT BROOKLYN COLLEGE

Flatbush and Nostrand Aves., Brooklyn; (718) 951-4500

Brooklyn College's enormous, 2,500-seat theater bustles nearly all year round with music, dance, and children's shows. From October to May, look for at least six professional presentations in ballet, modern/ contemporary, and ethnic dance as part of BC's subscription series. The theater also hosts student dance productions and rentals by dance companies. There is a mailing list, and subscribers receive discounts.

CITY CENTER THEATER

130 W. 56th St.; (212) 581-1212

City Center, the midtown dance space with neo-Moorish flourishes, is deceptively large—2,684 seats. Built in 1923 by a group of Shriners who wanted a clubhouse where they could smoke cigars, the building was purchased by New York City in 1943, turned into a concert hall, renamed City Center, and in 1976 redesigned as a dance house. In these post-dance boom days it also stages musical offerings. It's still home to the Alvin Ailey, Paul Taylor, and Merce Cunningham companies and regularly hosts visits by sizeable troupes like San Francisco Ballet and the Martha Graham Company. Subscribers receive information on upcoming events.

LEHMAN CENTER FOR THE PERFORMING ARTS

250 Bedford Boulevard West, Bronx; (718) 960-8833

With 2,322 seats, the spacious Lehman Center hosts a season of large-scale dance events, including visits by international ballet and folk dance troupes. Subscribers get events information—and discounts.

MAJESTIC THEATER

651 Fulton St., Brooklyn; (718) 636-4111 or (718) 636-4181

Opened in 1904 with a production of *The Wizard of Oz*, the 1,828-seat Majestic Theater for years was a tryout theater for Broadway-bound productions. It became a movie house in 1942, and in 1968, after almost being demolished, it was taken over by the city and linked with BAM, which helped form 651, the arts center housed in it. 651 has its own mailing list and often produces dance events, including dance/music collaborations.

METROPOLITAN OPERA HOUSE

30 Lincoln Plaza; (212) 362-6000

The Met's vast stage, 80 feet deep, is superb for opera, less so for ballet, particularly abstract works with small casts. Still, it's a handsome showcase for big story ballets presented by companies like Amercan Ballet Theater, Britain's Royal Ballet and the Kirov. Try not to sit too close; the third row, lovely for opera, is disastrous for watching ballet. Built in 1966, the opera house holds 4,000 people (3,800 in seats, 200 standing room); bring binoculars for any seat beyond Orchestra row O.

NEW YORK STATE THEATER

20 Lincoln Plaza; (212) 870-5570

The 2,729-seat jewel box, with lights that look like diamonds and side balconies shaped like a dancer's arms in first position, was designed to display ballet, and the care and planning shows. Nearly all the seats are good, even the upper rafters of heaven in the Fourth Ring (bring binoculars). And the sensible stage dimensions mean that a solo without scenery can look every bit as good as a big Balanchine piece, like *Symphony in C*. Home to the New York City Ballet, the State also occasionally hosts other companies, such as Dance Theater of Harlem and the Joffrey Ballet of Chicago.

∽ MIDDLE SIZE ∽

FLORENCE GOULD HALL

55 E. 59th St.; (212) 355-6160

Contemporary dance and small ballet companies often rent this attractive 400-seat theater when the Alliance Français is not using it to show French films.

JOYCE THEATER

175 Eighth Ave.; (212) 242-0800

Originally the Elgin Theater, a 1941 Art Deco-style movie house, the 472-seat Joyce was converted into a dance theater in 1982 as a resident performance space for Feld Ballets/NY, which dances in February, March, and August. Since its beginnings, more than 130 of the finest modern and contemporary companies have performed here. The annual Altogether Different series spotlights less established companies. Subscribers get advance notice of events and ticket discounts. Avoid the first row if possible—or bring a towel. Dance can be a sweaty business.

SYLVIA & DANNY KAYE PLAYHOUSE

695 Park Ave.; (212) 772-5207

Opened in 1993, and known as Kaye Playhouse, this handsome 624-seat theater hosts more than a dozen ballet and contemporary dance companies a year, including the Nikolais and Murray Louis Dance Company, the resident troupe. The stage is nicely scaled for dance, and the red velvet seats and curtain look appropriately theatrical. Mailing list members receive an events brochure.

PLAYHOUSE 91

316 E. 91st St.; (212) 831-2000

Handsomely refurbished, the 300-seat Playhouse presents dance programs produced by the 92nd Street Y Harkness Dance Center. Programs are part of a subscription series; you can also sign up for the mailing list.

SYMPHONY SPACE

2537 Broadway; (212) 864-5400

Local and international dance companies, mainly contemporary, visit this tired but homey 880-seat theater from 12 to 20 times a year. Most dance performances are one or two nights only. Symphony Space produces about 25 percent of its dance performances, and will alert dance fans who sign its mailing list. Information on troupes that rent the space is available at the box office or for members ($40 a year), who also get ticket discounts.

∼ PETITES ∼

CONTEXT STUDIOS

28 Avenue A; 505-2707

Dancers frequently rent this 80-seat studio as a theater which has no subscription or mailing list.

MERCE CUNNINGHAM DANCE STUDIO

55 Bethune St.; (212) 691-9751

This austerely sleek Westbeth space doubles as a studio for the Merce Cunningham company and as a popular rental performance space for small downtown contemporary companies. With its 55-person capacity and affordable price, performers rent it at least once a week. No subscription or mailing list. Caveat: visitors must remove their shoes.

DIA CENTER FOR THE ARTS
155 Mercer St.; (212) 431-9233
Dia's downtown space seats around 60 and is rented by contemporary dancers and other performers from September to June. No subscription or mailing list.

JUDSON MEMORIAL CHURCH
55 Washington Square South; (212) 477-0351 or 732-1227
In the 1960s, the 200-seat Judson Church was home to the ground-breaking experimental work of such choreographers as Trisha Brown, Yvonne Rainer, Simone Forti, and Steve Paxton. These days, the church has an arts program featuring occasional dance productions, including summer garden performances, all free. Movement Research, a dance services and support organization, also presents free dance performances on Monday nights at 8 p.m. Although most programs showcase new artists, established performers like Bebe Miller, Ralph Lemon, Douglas Dunn, and Wendy Peron have appeared recently.

THE KITCHEN CENTER FOR MUSIC AND VIDEO
512 W. 19th St.; (212) 255-5793
The Kitchen presents emerging dancers, musicians and performance artists but also provides space for established artists who don't require a large performance space. Begun in 1971 in SoHo, the Kitchen moved to Chelsea in 1985 and contains two "theaters" —downstairs seats around

125, upstairs about 100. Most performances are either fully or co-produced by the Kitchen, with only a few rentals each season. Discount tickets available with a subscription; there is also a mailing list.

LA MAMA EXPERIMENTAL THEATER CLUB
74 E. 4th St.; (212) 475-7710
La MaMa, with its 200-seat theater, produces around ten contemporary dance performances a year. Call to get on the mailing list and receive schedules.

OHIO THEATER
66 Wooster St.; (212) 966-4844
Run by SoHo Think Tank, this funky one-time hat factory can accommodate around 75 spectators for a performance. Downtown contemporary companies usually rent space, though Soho Think Tank produces a few presentations. Neo Labos is the resident company.

PERFORMANCE SPACE 122 (PS 122)
150 First Ave.;　(212) 477-5288
Opened in 1980, Performance Space 122 holds an audience of 100 to 250 and hosts frequent performances by downtown dance troupes and performance artists. Works are juried by PS 122 curators. There is a mailing list, and discounts are offered for subscribers.

ST. MARK'S CHURCH IN-THE-BOWERY
131 E. 10th St.;　(212) 674-8194
With its colonial pillars, big windows, and soft lighting, the main sanctuary of this landmark church is one of New York's most enchanting stages. And there's dancing much of the year, produced by the Danspace Project, begun in 1974 to provide affordable performance space for

independent experimental choreographers. Over the years, Danspace has shown some superb performers, both new and established. The organization produces and curates concerts 20 weeks a year and turns over the church for ten weeks of its EVENTS series, in which artists rent the space. There is a mailing list.

BESSIE SCHÖNBERG THEATER
219 W. 19th St.; (212) 924-0077
The 100-seat Bessie Shönberg theater, named for one of the dance world's most revered composition teachers, is modest but busy—hosting more than 200 contemporary dance, performance, and theater concerts a year. With the exception of a few June and August rentals, nearly every company is produced by Dance Theater Workshop, which has promoted small, independent cutting-edge troupes since 1965. Selections are juried, and the results, while occasionally uneven, can be superb. All told, a terrific place to check out what's new. Associate members (dues are $25 a year) receive ticket discounts.

SOLO ARTS GROUP INC. (SAGI)
36 W. 17th St.; (212) 463-8732
SAGI, a three-year-old production organization with a small Flatiron district space, shows finished dance works (no works-in-progress) by independent artists. A least 15 dance companies use SAGI's intimate space—it seats 30—each year. SAGI selects and produces the shows, and it has a mailing list for dance enthusiasts.

SQUID DANCE PERFORMANCE SPACE
127 Fulton St.; (212) 566-8041
This long, narrow studio run by dancers, including performer Roseanne Spradlin, has a new oak floor and seats about 50. Opened in November

1994, it is currently rented for performances, although its owners may eventually begin producing contemporary dance here as well.

THE THEATER AT RIVERSIDE CHURCH
490 Riverside Dr.; (212) 222-5900 or (212) 864-2929
Contemporary and modern solo performers and choreographers with small companies rent this 200-seat theater with a gold curtain and a smallish stage. (It's also used a lot for productions by Columbia and Barnard students.) No subscription and no mailing lists are available.

~ **CHAPTER TWO** ~

Home Town Troupes and Performers
. . . and Slightly Beyond

EVERYONE KNOWS THESE ARE HARD TIMES FOR DANCE, with decreased public and private funding and an audience that, sadly, has shrunk since the boom days of the 1970s and 1980s. Still, the more than 100 companies described in this plump chapter are just a fraction of the area's dance troupes and performers.

On almost any given night, dance enthusiasts have a dizzying choice, from contemporary companies and experimental soloists to folk dancers and master tappers. Try naming one other city with more ballet companies than New York. And where else can you find a resident ice dancing troupe, a company of concert ballroom dancers *and* the Rockettes?

These brief sketches will reacquaint you with familiar companies you've seen or plan to see, as well as pique your interest in artists you've never dreamed of seeing. Newspaper listings often mention dance companies simply by name, giving no details, so this chapter is designed to fill in the blanks by providing a brief synopsis of company history and dancing style and, occasionally, review snippets. Theaters frequented by each company are featured as well. Though the smallest ones don't have business phone numbers, you often can track down a company through a theater it recently visited.

Also included are a sampling of companies in Connecticut and New Jersey that are too good to ignore. They are just a short trip away—and are always eager to hit the road and perform in New York.

∼ BALLET COMPANIES ∼

ALVIN AILEY AMERICAN DANCE THEATER
211 W. 61st St.; (212) 767-0590

When Alvin Ailey started his school in 1969 as a training ground for his company, he put a diverse curriculum in place, including Horton, Dunham, and Graham-based modern dance techniques as well as ballet, tap, yoga, and West African dance. The resulting fluency with dance's varied languages quickly became a company trademark and strength. It also helped facilitate a seamless transition, when the magnificent dancer Judith Jamison took over as artistic director (Ailey died in 1989). From his company's modest start in 1958, the Texas-born Ailey envisioned a multicultural troupe that would dance significant works from the past as well as new pieces, his and others. Ailey created 79 ballets, including contemporary classics like *Blues Suite* and *Cry*, but also embraced works by over 50 choreographers, including signature pieces like John Butler's *Carmina Burana* and Donald McKayle's *Rainbow Round My Shoulder*. Known for bold, fearless dancing and a team of gracefully aggressive dancers, the company regularly packs in crowds at its annual City Center season.

AMERICAN BALLET THEATER (ABT)
890 Broadway; (212) 477-3030

After a rocky patch in the early 1990s, when this big, important company teetered toward bankruptcy, American Ballet Theater regained its footing and once again looks strong and reasonably solvent. And with a roster of superb dancers, budding stars like Paloma Herrera, and a confident artistic director, former ABT principal dancer Kevin McKenzie, the future of the one of the nation's oldest, finest, and most versatile ballet troupes seems bright. In 1995, ABT's annual season at the Met expanded from six to eight weeks, and the company is in demand for touring. ABT also is producing new ballets again, with recent works by Twyla Tharp, Lar Lubovitch, and James Kudelka. The company's great strength is its nimbleness. One night you'll see a full-length *Romeo and Juliet*, exquisitely danced with skillful acting, lavish costumes, and imposing sets. The next night, it's three one-acts, from plotless pieces by George Balanchine and Paul Taylor to expressionistic works by Antony Tudor and Agnes de Mille. ABT is also one of the remaining companies that proudly pushes the star system and unveils the cast list with great fanfare. And sleekly trained dancers like Susan Jaffe, Julie Kent, Amanda McKerrow, Alessandra Ferri, Julio Bocca, and more, the company that has been home to Makarova and Baryshnikov, Gregory and Bujones continues to dazzle.

BALLET FOR YOUNG AUDIENCES
243 W. 98th St.; (212) 662-4628
In the early 1980s, choreographer Harriet Kinter worked with a group
that presented theater productions for inner city young people. She
liked what she saw, and in 1982 started her own company for kids who
might otherwise never see ballet. The company presents hour-long
programs with music and narration, such as *Peter and the Wolf* for
elementary school kids. Middle-school kids see the company's
Nutcracker and *Sleeping Beauty*. And older students get longer, more
sophisticated works, such as *Romeo and Juliet*, choreographed by
Kinter. The troupe's 14 dancers, all soloists, are young, age 19 to 24;
most graduated from School of American Ballet, the Joffrey Ballet
School, and the Alvin Ailey American Dance Center. And they display
a range of body types and ethnic backgrounds. "Children need to see
that," Kinter says. Her troupe often performs at the 92nd Street Y,
Town Hall, and Symphony Space.

BRONX DANCE THEATER
286 E. 204th St., Bronx 10467; (718) 652-7655
The only company of its kind in the Bronx, the Bronx Dance Theater
presents several performances a year in its 250-seat theater, a 1927
movie house renovated for dance in 1987. Besides an annual *Nutcracker*, the small company has staged productions of *Coppelia*, *Swan
Lake* and original ballets based on Disney films, including *Beauty and
the Beast*. Dancers, mostly in their teens and early twenties, include
graduates of the High School of the Performing Arts and the Bronx
Dance Theater's school. The company, begun in 1976, also stages an
annual tap show in April and a jazz dance performance around
Halloween.

DANCE THEATER OF HARLEM (DTH)

466 West 152nd Street; (212) 690-2800

In 1994, the Dance Theater of Harlem celebrated its twenty–fifth anniversary with a glittery season at the New York State Theater and a roster of ballets—Alvin Ailey's *The River*, Glenn Tetley's *Voluntaries*, an exotic *Firebird* set in the Caribbean—that showed off this celebrated troupe's versatility and sizzle. The season was particularly triumphant, given the obstacles DTH faced during its first quarter century. Doubters claimed that classical dancing and African American body types did not mix, a notion quickly dropped once the dancers started *dancing*. And financial difficulties caused the company to shut down for six months in 1990. But these days, with 36 well-trained dancers, including the divine Virginia Johnson, a generous repertory of over 75 works, and numerous touring engagements, Dance Theater of Harlem is flourishing. It began humbly in 1968, when founder Arthur Mitchell, the New York City Ballet's first African American principal dancer, abandoned a thriving ballet career to start a dance school for Harlem kids. He launched the company a year later and established its signature mix of classical and neoclassical works with contemporary dances, nearly all freshened with African American themes (his Creole *Giselle* is a company classic).

DANCES PATRELLE

126 4th Place, Brooklyn 11231; (718) 802-0187

Not many choreographers are interested in creating full-scale narrative ballets these days, but Francis Patrelle, a choreographer and teacher, does little else. "I'm passionate about dramatic dance," he says. And practicing what he preaches, Patrelle has carved a niche for himself and his company, which performs each spring at Kaye Playhouse. Besides being a showcase for his work, Patrelle's company, launched in 1988, has become a showcase for some of New York's finest dancers, among them New York City Ballet's Merrill, Ashley and Judith Fugate, American Ballet Theater's Wes Chapman, and freelancers Medhi Bahiri and Leda Meredith. Cynthia Gregory, the longtime ABT star, gave her farewell performance in Patrelle's *Clara*, a 20-minute ode to pianst Clara Schumann. Though Patrelle makes mixed bills of short pieces, his heart belongs to evening-length works—chamber versions of *Romeo and Juliet*, *The Firebird*, and, recently, *Macbeth*, as dramatic as can be.

THE DARING PROJECT

Russian-born ballerina Valentina Kozlova retired from New York City Ballet in 1995, but not from the dance world. Her new troupe, the Daring Company, made its New York debut in July 1995 and has since appeared at the Newport Festival in East Hampton. Her company's first production, *From Ballet to Broadway*, neatly sums up Kozlova's career since her 1979 defection from the Soviet Union, where she was a Bolshoi Ballet principal dancer. In 1982, Kozlova danced on Broadway in a revival of *On Your Toes*. A year later she joined New York City Ballet. Her new troupe, comprising mainly dancers from NYCB and American Ballet Theater, dances everything from classical pas de deux to contemporary ballet. Kozlova's collaborator, Margo Sappington, also creates jazzy dances for the troupe.

FELD BALLETS/NY

890 Broadway; (212) 777-7710

Out with the old seems the unofficial motto for Eliot Feld and his lively company, Feld Ballets/NY. "I want to engage my eye, and my eye is easily bored," Feld remarked when asked why he didn't stage a retrospective to celebrate his troupe's twentieth anniversary in 1994. Instead, he did what he does almost every season—created three new works, including *MRI*, with an airborne pas de deux that kept principals Lynn Aaron and Darren Gibson suspended from horizontal bars high above the stage. Feld's inventive dances inevitably tweak the boundaries of ballet, and his superb collection of dancers, with a diverse range of body types, are skillful tweakers, fluent in Feld's sinewy, jazzy vocabulary. (The rep is 100 percent Feld; he's made over 80 ballets.) Born in Brooklyn, Feld seems the ultimate New York choreographer, alert to the city's rhythms, wit, and street smarts. His resume includes stints with New York City Ballet (as the Prince in Balanchine's first *The Nutcracker*), Pearl Lang, Mary Anthony, and Donald McKayle, and American Ballet Theater. You can glimpse him, blond and still skinny, as Baby John in the movie of *West Side Story*. And you can catch his company at its Joyce Theater home in late summer and late winter.

ILYA GAFT DANCE THEATER
167 W. 46th St.; (212) 730-6933
This small, serious company with eight core members and assorted guest soloists specializes in classical ballet at its purest. Artistic director Ilya Gaft danced with the Leningrad Opera and Ballet Theater and taught at Russia's Vagonava State Choreographic Institute. He favors dramatic dance that touches emotions and tells a story rather than movement for its own sake. His company, which has danced at Merkin Concert Hall and numerous schools, performs classics and contemporary ballets as well as ballets for children.

MANHATTAN BALLET COMPANY
1556 Third Ave.; (212) 369-3369
This small company, built around a core of the Manhattan Ballet School's best teenage dancers, performs twice a year at schools through-

out New York City. In the winter, the troupe dances *The Nutcracker*. In the spring, they dance a mixture of classics, usually excerpts from *Giselle*, *Coppelia*, and similar works. To round out the roster, artistic director Elfriede Merman usually recruits dancers from New York City Ballet, the Joffrey Ballet, and other prominent companies.

NEW CHOREOGRAPHERS ON POINT/BALLET BUILDERS
355 E. 72nd St.; (212) 861-9619

New Choreographers on Point was formed in 1991 to give fledgling ballet choreographers an opportunity—and a stage—to show off new work. And so far, the company has won praise for its enthusiastic, if uneven, results. Choreographers audition for inclusion in each presentation, called Ballet Builders. The company's fifth season in spring 1995 featured seven choreographers, who presented works at the Clark Studio Theater in Lincoln Center's Rose Building, among them former New York City Ballet soloist, Jean-Pierre Frohlich; Carlos Fittante, co-director of Balinese American Fusion Dance; and Tassia Hooks of Dance Theater of Harlem. Dancers from the Joffrey Ballet, Eleo Pomare Dance Company, Atlanta Ballet, and Ballet Hispanico have also performed. Choreography is contemporary, both barefoot and on point, but always fluent in the vocabuary of classical ballet.

NEW YORK CITY BALLET (NYCB)
20 Lincoln Center; (212) 870-5500

With over 100 magnificently trained dancers, a 23-week New York season, and a repertory stocked with more than 100 adventurous ballets, New York City Ballet is widely viewed as the gold standard among dance companies. For many New Yorkers, ballet would be unimaginable without NYCB's two long seasons at the New York State Theater, starting with *The Nutcracker* in November. The rep veers from the neoclassical, music-driven works of founding artistic director George Balanchine to Jerome Robbins's witty, theatrical dances, and it seems oddly timeless. Indeed, the three Balanchine ballets danced at NYCB's first performance in 1948—*Concerto Barocco, Symphony in C,* and *Orpheus*—are still in the rep. And the dancers performing them are among finest, *fastest,* and most exciting in the world, from classic Balanchine ballerinas Kyra Nichols and Darci Kistler to a dynamic team of men, led by Damien Woetzel and Jock Soto. Under artistic director Peter Martins, the majestic Danish dancer who took over following Balanchine's death in 1983, the company has suffered a few setbacks but has always bounced back, innovative and strong. Regular infusions of new choreography, including the bienniel Diamond Project, show off the dancers' versatility and have kept the company contemporary. And a crew of young daredevils, Ethan Stiefel and Jenifer Ringer among them, ensures that NYCB's future should be as splendid as its past.

NEW YORK THEATER BALLET
30 E. 31st St.; (212) 679-0401
Since 1977, the New York Theater Ballet has occupied a niche as New York City's chamber ballet company, even if chamber ballet, as critic Jennifer Dunning once pointed out, seems a contradiction in terms. Classical ballet, almost by definition, is performed on big stages with opera-size casts. Yet company founder and artistic director Diana Byer and her ten-member troupe have devised a successful formula, presenting small-scale works by such master choreographers as Michel Fokine, Anton Dolin, and Antony Tudor as well as original contemporary pieces. The company also performs hour-length adaptations of classics, like *Cinderella,* for children. The company's regular New York seasons include an annual *Nutcracker* at Florence Gould Hall.

STATEN ISLAND BALLET

3081 Richmond Rd., Staten Island 10306; (718) 980-0500

Just three years old, the Staten Island Ballet, New York City's regional company, is still something of a secret. But this plucky troupe, engaging from 18 to 25 dancers, thinks big. Artistic director Ellen Tharp, formerly of Manhattan Ballet Company, hired a 51-piece orchestra for last year's production of *The Nutcracker*. And the current schedule calls for four full productions a season, mostly mixed bills choreographed by Tharp. Starting a new company in New York City wasn't all that difficult, Tharp says. "There's a huge pool of unemployed talent in the area." Advertisements on a Russian cable television station attracted former members of the Bolshi, Kirov, and Georgia State Ballet companies. For now, home base is the impressive performing arts center of the College of Staten Island.

$\sim$ MODERN AND CONTEMPORARY DANCE $\sim$ GROUPS AND PERFORMERS

ALPHA-OMEGA THEATRICAL DANCE COMPANY

For a recent season at Marymount Manhattan Theater, Alpha-Omega danced to works by five African American choreographers, including modern-dance master Eleo Pomare and Tony award winner George Faison, known for devising memorable concert and video appearances for Natalie Cole and Stevie Wonder. The evening showed the versatility of this proudly multicultural company, begun in 1972, which specializes in vibrant, dramatic dance, from modern to Broadway.

MARY ANTHONY DANCE THEATER

736 Broadway; (212) 674-8191

With her dance school dating from 1954 and her company from 1956,

Mary Anthony quietly helped shape the look and style of modern dance. A student of choreographer Hanya Holm, and later a member of her company, Anthony performed in concerts, appeared on Broadway and danced briefly on television in the 1950s with other young moderns, among them Bertram Ross, Jane Dudley, and Paul Taylor. For Anthony, movement is always linked with an emotional impulse. Her lyrical, carefully crafted dances, with an undercurrent of simplicity, impart a range of strong emotions. Recent works, performed at the Cunningham Studio, include *Requiem*, about the power of faith and hope (the music is Gabriel Fauré's), and the abstract Seascape, to music by Debussy, Nicholas Milosevich, and John La Montane.

BALINESE AMERICAN FUSION DANCE
23 W. 35th St.; (212) 563-9111
As its name says, Balinese American Fusion Dance deliberately blends the aesthetics of Eastern and Western cultures in its repertory of over 20 works. Specifically, the company fuses traditional Balinese movement, concentrated largely on the hands, eyes, and torso, with looser Western dance movements. Dances, choreographed by founder Islene Pinder and artistic director Carlos Fittante, are usually performed in elaborate Balinese-inspired headdresses, masks, and makeup. The company has danced in New York at festivals like Lincoln Center Out–of–Doors, and the Downtown Dance Festival.

NANETTE BEARDEN CONTEMPORARY DANCE THEATER
357 Canal St.; (212) 966-6828
Nanette Bearden began her repertory company in 1976 to concentrate on works by new and established African American choreographers. A recent performance at Marymount Manhattan Theater featured two works by the late Talley Beatty, set to music by Miles Davis and Earth,

Wind and Fire, as well as Steven Simien's *Elegy for a Lady* to music by Billie Holliday. The rep blends ballet, jazz, and modern dance, neatly reflecting Bearden's background. The widow of artist Romare Bearden—illustrations by Bearden often grace program announcements—she studied at the Martha Graham School and the Luigi Dance Center, and designed her troupe to showcase works by young dancers and choreographers.

ROBIN BECKER & COMPANY
(212) 316-2958

Robin Becker gets ideas for her delicate, lyrical dances from paintings, poetry, and music. The 13th-century mystical Persian poet Rumi provided imagery for two vignettes of *Dances from Rumi*, which deftly translates verbal imagery into motion. And *Prayer* is a meditative solo based on a Rodin sculpture and danced by Becker. Becker's expressionistic, often powerful dances offer hints at her background. Born in Chicago, she danced with Martha Graham and Eleo Pomare. Her troupe has danced at St. Mark's Church, Playhouse 91, and the Joyce Theater.

LORI BELILOVE & COMPANY
141 W. 26th St.; (212) 691-5040

Though every dance aficionado knows about Isadora Duncan, for years many weren't entirely certain what her dances looked like. But since the 1978 centennial of Duncan's birth, Duncan companies have sprouted up all over New York. Lori Belilove's company, formed in 1988, is one of the most professional. Like Duncan, Belilove was born in San Francisco. In sensitively restaging works from 1900 to 1923, Belilove has melded Duncan's movement philosophy with a contemporary vision. She also has choreographed new works for her troupe in the

Duncan spirit. The company's Duncan rep, performed in its Chelsea studio, includes works set to music by Chopin, Brahms, Schubert, and Tchaikovsky, among others.

BEVERLY BLOSSOM

(212) 953-0651

"Eloquently nutty" is how a *New York Times* critic described one of Beverly Blossom's recent solo works, and it's hard to disagree. Dancer-actress Blossom, a principal dancer with Alwin Nikolais from 1953 to 1963, creates fanciful, exuberant solos and performs them handily in concert at places like Marymount Manhattan Theater. In *Besame Mucho*, she tangos, dips, and indulges in dance hall dramatics, dressed on one side as a gigolo and on the other in a slinky pink 1930s gown.

RON BROWN/EVIDENCE

P.O. Box 20389, London Terrace Station, New York 10011
(718) 636-8180

Ron Brown studied with Mary Anthony and Bessie Schönberg and danced with Jennifer Muler/The Works. But his athletic, expressionistic choreography is all his own—and never abstract. The result is original, loosely narrative, issue-driven dance dealing with subjects like race, class, gender, and assimilation. He choreographed *Evidence*, an early work about growing up black, after the death of a favorite uncle. *Dirt Road*, a recent evening-length piece set to gospel and pop music, is a generational drama of a black family, touching issues of poverty, injustice and resilience. His company has performed at the Joyce Theater and St. Mark's Church. In 1994, *The New York Times* selected Brown as one of 30 artists under the age 30 most likely to change the culture in the next 30 years.

TRISHA BROWN COMPANY

225 Lafayette St.; (212) 334-9374

By the mid-1960s, Trisha Brown had made a name for herself as one of the most innovative abstract choreographers of the now–legendary Judson Dance Theater. Brown, who formed her current company in 1970, is still a formidable dancer and choreographer, known for structural rigor and supple kineticism. She seems equally comfortable working on a large and a small scale. Several recent pieces have been grand theatrical works, created in collaboration with eminent artists and musicians like Donald Judd, Nancy Graves, Laurie Anderson, John Cage, and Robert Rauschenberg. But Brown still makes intimate pieces, like a recent solo, *If You Couldn't See Me*, which she danced, start to finish, with her back to the audience. The work showed that expression in dance comes from the torso, pelvis, and limbs, not the face. Look for her company's frequent seasons at places like the Joyce Theater and City Center.

DONALD BYRD/THE GROUP

59 Franklin St.; (212) 431-7362

Donald Byrd's choreography is eclectic: recent efforts ranged from a study in domestic violence inspired by the theatrical theories of Brecht to an African American interpretation of *The Nutcracker*, set to Duke Ellington's jazzy take on Tchaikovsky. The eclecticism is deliberate— Byrd's goal is to create works that affect many people. His background in ballet and modern dance is also eclectic; he danced with Twyla Tharp, Karole Armitage, and Gus Solomons jr. His own company, formed in 1978 in Los Angeles, moved to New York in 1983. The rep ranges from abstract dances to works addressing social issues, all with a movement vocabulary that integrates black vernacular dance with ballet and modern techniques. The troupe has danced at the Joyce Theater, 92nd Street Y, and Brooklyn's Majestic Theater.

CHEN & DANCERS
70 Mulberry St.; (212) 349-2026
American modern dance and traditional Asian dance and theatrics come together in almost equal parts in the stylized, story-based dances of H. T. Chen. Formed in 1978, this mostly Asian American troupe neatly reflects Chen's personal history. Born in Shanghai and raised in Taiwan, he studied at Juilliard and the Martha Graham School and spent five years immersed in experimental theater at La MaMa. Resulting works include *Double Happiness*, *100 Sorrows*, centered on marriage in Asian cultures, and *Hidden Voices*, the true story of Chinese immigrants recruited as strikebreakers in a 19th-century Massachusetts factory. The company has performed at Dance Theater Workshop, Riverside Church Dance Festival, and LaMama.

LUCINDA CHILDS DANCE COMPANY
Lucinda Childs' pristine, minimalist choreography is the dance equivalent of an Agnes Martin painting or a Sol Lewitt sculpture. Appropriately, she collaborated with Lewitt and composer Philip Glass on *Dance*, a large-scale, evening-length work of 1979. Childs, an alum of the Judson Dance Theater, formed her company in 1973 and has choreographed on very large and very small scales. On the large side was her collaboration with Robert Wilson on his 1976 opera, *Einstein on the Beach*, in which she danced intensely cerebral pieces, full of repetitive structures. Among her smaller works is *One and One*, a surprisingly sensual dance set to compositions by Greek-French composer Iannis Xenakis. The ten–dancer company, with its repertory of over 25 works, turns up periodically in New York at places like the Joyce Theater.

YOSHIKO CHUMA & THE SCHOOL OF HARD KNOCKS
201 E. 4th St.; (212) 533-9473

Rapscallion vaudville is the term critic Marcia B. Siegel used to describe experimental choreographer Yoshiko Chuma's dances a while back, and it's hard to disagree. A case in point: *Crash Orchestra*, which explores the physical and emotional relationship between dance and music, musician and instrument. The energetic mixed–media work features 14 performers who dance, play instruments, and sing, creating continuous movement and sound. Japan's 1960s counterculture movement was a big influence on Chuma's work, which combines elements of street theater, spontaneity and eccentricity. Chuma and her company have performed at the Joyce Theater, Dance Theater Workshop, the Kitchen, and PS 122, among other places.

JANE COMFORT & COMPANY
(212) 226-5109

Jane Comfort is a familiar, well-respected presence in New York's downtown performance world, known for dance-theater pieces that address contemporary social, psychological, and political issues. Her recent evening-length *S/he* took on the gender wars, with characters that included a voluptuous Barbie, a battered wife played by a man, and Anita Hill and Clarence Thomas—with Thomas portrayed by a domineering woman. Comfort, who choreographed Stephen Sondheim's recent musical *Passion*, deftly uses spoken text as the basis for her choreography. A native of Oak Ridge, Tennessee, Comfort has performed in New York at Lincoln Center's Serious Fun festival, PS 122, and Dance Theater Workshop.

COLIN CONNOR
(212) 871-8676

Born in London and raised in Canada, Colin Connor didn't start dancing until he was 22. Since then, he's performed with the Mary Anthony Dance Theater and the José Limón Dance Company, where he was a soloist for eight years. In 1981, he formed his own company to present his vigorous, well-crafted dances. Rhythmically wedded to the music and full of bold movement, Connor's dances explore dramatic or emotional content. They can also be witty. The dancers in *The Rye Catchers*, set to Henry Purcell's arrangements of 17th-century tavern songs, swagger around the stage in mini-kilts. Connor has created works for the Carolyn Dorfman Dance Company and City College of New York, and most recently performed in New York at the Cunningham Studio.

COYOTE DANCERS
131 Thompson St.; (212) 505-2525

Dancer Maher Benham currently teaches at the Martha Graham School and Graham's influence comes through clearly in the stretches, contractions, and swirls performed by Benham's Coyote Dancers. Formed in 1993, the troupe frequently features former Graham performers like Stuart Hodes, a favorite Graham partner in the 1950s. Benham, who has danced with Pearl Lang, Daniel Maloney, and the Graham Company, gets polished performances from her dancers. And her works can be unusual. Her September 1995 season at Kaye Playhouse featured two large-scale works—17 men, from teens to septuagenerians, danced *Sipapu*, which means eternal life force in Apache, while twelve women appeared in *Night of Light*, a study in sisterhood and community.

CREACH/KOESTER

(212) 924-5443

Terry Creach and Stephen Koester have danced together since 1980, creating highly physical yet witty pieces for male dancers. Their work, performed at New York University's Tisch School of the Arts and the Ohio Theater, focuses on the physical possibililities of men dancing as well as various relationships between men. The pair, who often collaborate with composers, dance as part of their six-man troupe.

MERCE CUNNINGHAM DANCE COMPANY

55 Bethune St.; (212) 691-9751

In 1989, when he was almost 70, Merce Cunningham became one of the first choreographers to make dances on a computer. In a *Newsweek* interview, he declared he wasn't doing anything revolutionary. "It's exactly like Petipa," he said, noting that the great 19th-century ballet choreographer moved around cut-out dolls when creating new dances. But the computer seems the perfect medium for Cunningham, one of the first choreographers to emphasize pure movement over music, story, and emotion. In his pre-computer days, he often tossed a coin or threw dice to determine a sequence of movements.

With nearly 200 slyly witty dances, Cunningham is one of the century's leading movement artists. And he's still going strong, creating vibrant new works for his company's annual City Center season. After an early career dancing with the Martha Graham Company, he started his troupe in 1953 and collaborated over the years with great contemporary artists, including Robert Rauschenberg, Frank Stella, Andy Warhol, Jasper Johns, Robert Morris, and composer John Cage. His beautifully trained dancers display all hallmarks of the Cunningham technique—strength, clarity, and precision. Cunnnigham's immaculate white studio is also a popular small performance space.

LAURA DEAN MUSICIANS AND DANCERS

295 Greenwich St.; (212) 732-1148

Laura Dean's company is aptly named. Since she formed it in 1973, Dean has choreographed dances *and* composed original scores for all but five of the 20-some works in her rep. A former member of the Paul Taylor Dance Company (she still teaches at Taylor's school), she has impeccable modern dance credentials. But Dean is perhaps best known as a choreographer for ballet companies, notably the Royal Danish Ballet, New York City Ballet, and the Joffrey (her *Sometimes It Snows in April*, to music by Prince, was a sensation in the Joffrey's *Billboards*). Dean's abstract work is marked by repeated phrases, energetic intensity, and a deliberately reductive vocabulary. Look for her company at the Joyce Theater.

DAVID DORFMAN DANCE

David Dorfman lettered in football and baseball in high school and never completely abandoned the trappings of a jock. In performance pieces that have taken him all over the world—as well as to the Kitchen, St. Mark's Church, and the Joyce Theater—he melds risky athletic movement with choreography that frequently explores the male psyche, often humorously. He also mixes monologues with his moves (he's been called the Spalding Grey of choreography). In *Out of Season, the Athletes Project*, Dorfman and his six-person company rehearse for three weeks with a group of volunteer athletes from local communities where they tour. The athletes help shape Dorfman's choreography and appear on stage in the finished creation.

DUNCAN DANCE CONTINUUM

75 East End Ave.; (212) 772-3963

In 1993, Judith Landon, a long-time Duncan-style dancer, formed

Duncan Dance Continuum to present reconstructions of the full Isadora Duncan's repertoire, from 1900 to 1922. The ten-member company, which often dances at the Theater of Riverside Church, performs barefoot in the Duncan tradition. Their recent performances have included *Marche Militaire* to music by Franz Schubert (seen for the first time since the 1920s) and the 1905 *Blue Danube Waltz*. The group has also danced reconstructions of Doris Humphrey's earliest dances.

DOUGLAS DUNN & DANCERS

Douglas Dunn began his career performing with Yvonne Rainer & Group (1968–70), the Merce Cunningham Dance Company (1969–73), and Grand Union (1970–76), a collective that included Trisha Brown, David Gordon, Steve Paxton, and Rainer. He also experimented with his own work, creating his company in 1977. His early work was about movement, but along the way, he infused it with allusions to emotion, characters, and situation. Dunn's witty unpredictability leaves audiences uncertain what to expect from his very good dancers. Sets and music play a large part in his highly theatrical pieces, and he routinely collaborates with visual artists, filmmakers and composers. In New York, Dance Theater Workshop has showcased his company.

EIKO & KOMA

It comes as no surprise to learn that Eiko & Koma's first teachers were Kazuo Ono and Tatsumi Hijikata, leading figures in butoh, Japan's postwar avant-garde dance/theater. But while works by the Japanese-born duo move with butoh's studied slowness, they also display serenity and beauty instead of butoh's darkness and nihilism. A mountain of feathers gently rain onto the stage in *Wind*, a mysterious 1993 evening-length piece performed by Eiko, Koma, and a small boy. Before settling in New York in 1976, the pair traveled through Europe and studied with

Mary Wigman disciple Manja Chmiel in Germany. They've appeared frequently at Japan Society and BAM and hold periodic Delicious Movement Workshops, dealing with movement vocabulary and performance techniques.

DOUG ELKINS DANCE COMPANY

P.O. Box 856, Peck Slip Station, New York 10272; (212) 785-6739

Doug Elkins likes to describe himself as a postmodern bagman. "I take inspiration for my dances from the way everyone moves—martial artists, my three-year-old nephew, great choreographers, club dancers," he says. And this mixed bag of influences is on view in his witty dances. To a score that blends music of James Brown, Handel, and Led Zeppelin, dancers in *More Wine for Polyphemus* flit from vogueing and break dancing to ballet. Elkins, who choreographed a music video for jazz saxophonist David Sanborn, frequently collaborates with composers. His company has danced at Dance Theater Workshop, Brooklyn's Majestic Theater, and the Joyce Theater.

GARTH FAGAN DANCE

50 Chestnut St., Rochester 14604; (716) 454-3260

Though based upstate in Rochester, Garth Fagan's 14-member company gets an enthusiastic New York City following for performances at places like the Joyce Theater. At the helm of his company since 1970, the Jamaican-born choreographer uses his own dance technique, drawn from the sense of weight in modern dance, the torso-centered energy of Afro-Caribbean dance, the speed and precision of ballet, and the experimentation of the postmoderns. The resulting work has a sharply geometric look garnished with "snarls and tangles," as critic Jack Anderson puts it. Fagan's dances are witty and forceful, often with unexpected twists; his *Never Top 40 (Juke Box)* from 1985 unfolds to an improbable mix of jazz, an operatic aria, and musical versions of the Psalms.

MOLISSA FENLEY

On the opening night of her 1995 season at the Joyce Theater, Molissa Fenley experienced every dancer's nightmare—she suffered a serious ligament injury during her third dance, and the performance, along with her entire Joyce season, was cancelled. The injury was doubly distressing, because Fenley had danced "splendidly and vigorously," critic Anna Kisselgoff wrote. Fenley, who formed her company in 1977 and became a solo performer in 1980, has long been one of dance's most intriguing experimental choreographers. Rapid turns and hip-swinging undulations fill her work. Born in Las Vegas and raised in Ibadan, Nigeria, she collaborates with high-profile downtown artists and musicians, among them Richard Serra, Richard Long, and Francesco Clemente. And Philip Glass has provided live piano accompaniment for two of her best-known solos, *Place* and *The Floor Dances*.

MIMI GARRARD DANCE THEATER
155 Wooster St.; (212) 674-6868

A variety of components—movement, music, and lighting—go into Mimi Garrard's witty dances for seven to nine performers. Before forming her troupe in 1965, Garrard danced with the Alwin Nikolais and Murray Louis companies. And her work displays hints of Nikolais's love of German expressionism and multimedia. Garrard, whose company recently danced at Theater of Riverside Church, gives careful attention to lighting, with special effects devised on a computer by her husband, artist James Seawright. In her 1970 *Phosphones*, computer–controlled pulses of light isolate dancers, causing them to appear and disappear within intricate rhythms of sound and color.

ANNABELLE GAMSON DANCE COMPANY

For more than 20 years, Annabelle Gamson has centered her career on historical modern dance. In the mid 1970s, Gamson reconstructed and performed the solo dances of Isadora Duncan, working with Julia Levien, a lifelong friend of Duncan's. She similarly researched the work of modern dance pioneer Mary Wigman, studying old films and consulting with Wigman disciple, Hanya Holm. When Gamson stopped performing in the mid–1980s, she began researching the dances of the 1930s and 1940s, interpreting them in clever, new abstract works, like *The Women of Union Square*, performed a couple of years ago at St. Mark's Church.

DAVID GORDON/PICK UP CO.

131 Varick St.; (212) 627-1213

As the lines between contemporary dance and performance blur, a number of choreographers have eased away from dance and embraced theater. Few have done this as thoroughly as David Gordon, whose most recent piece, *The Family Business*, a collaboration with his son, Ain Gordon, was presented at both Dance Theater Workshop *and* New York Theater Workshop. In the 1960s, Gordon and his dancer/actress wife, Valda Setterfield, were part of dance's experimental mainstream. After stints performing with James Waring and Yvonne Rainer, Gordon presented abstract works at the Judson Church. Along the way, he began using text and adding narrative content. But hints of his dance sensibility remain in the timing and fluidity of his theatrical pieces.

MARTITA GOSHEN'S EARTHWORKS

(516) 759-3676

Concern with the environment is an undercurrent of Martita Goshen's complex theatrical pieces, part contemporary dance, part performance.

Goshen's resume is long and unusual. A diplomat's daughter born in Montevideo, Uruguay, she worked as a teacher and staff assistant to Senator Robert F. Kennedy. She was also a world–class skier whose hopes to compete in the 1964 Olympics were dashed by a serious skiing accident. After extensive surgery and a plastic knee, she turned to dance. Goshen subsequently trained with José Limón, Anna Sokolow, Twyla Tharp, and Pilobolus and in 1981 formed Earthworks. Her complex, evening–length pieces, presented at places like St. Mark's Church, incorporate dance, text, and live music and create a mood rather than tell a story.

ZVI GOTHEINER & DANCERS
550 Broadway; (212) 925-1466
Born in Israel and raised on a kibbutz, Zvi Gotheiner learned his craft in his native country before setting up his ten-member, New York-based company in 1983. Gotheiner, whose work combines elements of ballet, modern dance, and folk motifs, creates theatrical, musical dances with strong elements of emotion and expressiveness. *Fragile*, a 1994 piece, deals with loneliness and longing as it unfolds in 19 segments, set to a diverse score that includes music by Johann Strauss and Miles Davis. His company has performed at the Joyce Theater, Cunningham Studio, and Lincoln Center Out-of-Doors.

MARTHA GRAHAM DANCE COMPANY
316 E. 63rd St.; (212) 832-9166
Everything about Martha Graham was a little larger than life. And her powerhouse company, which lost none of its artistic vigor after her death in 1991, seems larger than life, too. Formed in 1926, it is the oldest dance company in America. The cream of the dance world have performed with it, from Merce Cunningham, Pearl Lang, Elisa Monte, Paul Taylor, and

Erick Hawkins to eager ballet-world guest artists, like Mikhail Baryshnikov, Margot Fonteyn, and Rudolf Nureyev. The repertory of 181 works is pure Graham, from early works like *Heretic* (1929) to pieces composed in her nineties. In between are literally dozens of modern dance classics—*Primitive Mysteries*, *El Penitente*, *Appalachian Spring*, *Night Journey*, *Clytemnestra*, and *Seraphic Dialogue*.

Graham's life stretched across modern dance's juiciest history. Raised in California, she studied and taught at the Denishawn school, became a company member in 1919, and formed her own company seven years later. Graham blazed theatrical trails, as well, collaborating with composers like Louis Horst, Aaron Copland, and Gian Carlo Menotti and with sculptor Isamu Noguchi. Even photographs of her taken by Barbara Morgan and Imogen Cunningham are memorable, all those dramatically lit images of her sleek black hair, blood-red mouth, and that unforgettable *joli/laid* face.

ERICK HAWKINS DANCE COMPANY
375 West Broadway; (212) 226-5363

Erick Hawkins, one of modern dance's true originals, died in 1994 at the age of 85, but his company is alive and well. The choreographer left more than 50 works and an able troupe well schooled in his so-called free–flow technique. Using a metronome, Hawkins devised movements set to beats; the music came after the piece was done. The result was dances, performed barefoot, of extreme purity and clarity.

Hawkins's life story reads like a mini-history of 20th-century American dance. Born in Colorado, he danced in the original production of George Balanchine's *Serenade*, then moved on to become Martha Graham's first male soloist—he created signature roles in *Appalachian Spring* and *El Penitente*—and, briefly, Graham's husband. His company, formed in 1951, dances only Hawkins's works, set to live music created specially for the troupe by composers like Virgil Thomson, Alan Hovhaness, and Lucia Dlugoszewski, Hawkins's long-time companion. Recorded music is verboten. When Dlugoszewski's score for *Many Thanks*, one of Hawkins' s last works, remained unfinished at the work's premiere, the dance was performed in silence, quite successfully. One unperformed work, choreographed just before Hawkins's death, remains, and may eventually be presented at a company season at the Joyce Theater.

INFINITY DANCE THEATER

(212) 877-3490

This new company, which made its New York debut at the 1995 Mobility Junction Dance Festival, comprises professional dancers with and without physical disabilities—both in and out of wheelchairs. Its style is neatly summed up by the backgrounds of its three founders, Broadway dancer Christopher Lunn, jazz and classical dancer/teacher Robert Koval, and Kitty Lunn, a former soloist with the Washington National Ballet who became a paraplegic eight years ago when she slipped on ice and broke her back. (Though wheelchair bound, Lunn spent three years on *As the World Turns*.) The rep incorporate hints of Broadway, jazz, modern, and ballet.

ANDREW JANNETTI & DANCERS

P.O. Box 350, Prince Street Station, New York 10012
(212) 431-7313

A choreographer since 1981, dancer Andrew Jannetti and his seven-member troupe perform contemporary works built on form and movement with an undercurrent of emotion. Jannetti's dances range from playful and rhythmical to introspective, always with sculptural touches. The Philadelphia-born choreographer has danced with Claire Porter and Mimi Garrard, among others.

RISA JAROSLOW & DANCERS
65 Greene St.; (212) 941-9358

"I have always been interested in the ability of dance to explore and illuminate the dimensions of human relationships," says Risa Jaroslow. And Jaroslow's sensual, well-crafted works usually do precisely that. Jaroslow's choreographic themes touch upon intergenerational relationships, Jewish identity, immigration experiences, and women's issues. Her poignant 1995 dance/theater piece, *Book Song Woman Man*, for example, explores the tradition of study in Jewish life as well as the joys and sadnesses of youth and old age. Her company has danced at Joyce Theater and with Dancing in the Streets.

BILL T. JONES/ARNIE ZANE DANCE COMPANY
(212) 477-1850

In more than 20 years as a dancer and choreographer, Bill T. Jones has tweaked audiences with powerful, expressionistic dances that touch upon a range of social issues, from racism and gender identity to terminal illness. He also has moved gracefully between grand-scale, multimedia works to solos and small pieces. In the summer of 1995, he created an intriguing but modest duet for himself and experimental dance doyenne Trisha Brown, called *You Can See Us*, with a score, played backward and forward simultaneously, by artist Robert Rauschenberg. It followed the huge splash made by his controversial 1994 evening-length piece, *Still/Here*, a vast multimedia production (performed at BAM) based on the experiences of people who survived serious illness. This proudly multiracial troupe features a fascinating range of body types, from willowy Odile Reine-Adelaide to sumo-like Lawrence Goldhuber, all used by Jones to great effect.

PHYLLIS LAMHUT
225 W. 71st St.; (212) 799-9048

Phyllis Lamhut has been an active, and influential, member of the modern dance community for over 40 years, both as a dancer and choreographer. A longtime student of Alwin Nikolais, she was a principal dancer with his company for 20 years, danced with the Murray Louis Dance Company, and in 1970 started her own troupe. As a dancer, she was known for her sensitivity and wit. As a choreographer, she produces meticulously crafted, highly kinetic works built around social issues. *Dislocations*, from 1993, deals with joblessness. And *Man*, from 1989, was a response to the AIDS crisis. The company, which performs with live musicians, has danced at the Bessie Schönberg Theater.

RICHARD LEMON
P.O. Box 143, New York 10011

With his shaved head and graceful limbs, Ralph Lemon cuts a striking figure. His elegant, abstract dances, with a strong sense of symmetry and order, are equally striking. Until recently, his seven-member company, seen at places like Joyce Theater and St. Mark's Church, was the prime showcase for his evolving choreographic style. But in October 1995, Lemon disbanded the company, though he still plans to make dances. Lemon's work changed sharply around 1985, when he switched from narrative to abstract work. *Their Eyes Rolled Back in Ecstasy*, a prime example, explores movement against a background of Gregorian chants and music by ex-Pink Floyd Syd Barret, and Chris Hyams Hart—all played simultaneously.

LIMÓN DANCE COMPANY

611 Broadway; (212) 777-3353

Company founder José Limón died in 1972, but his troupe lost none of its vitality after his death. In the last two decades, more than 50 works by a panoply of top modern choreograhers—Murray Louis, Kurt Jooss, Annabelle Gamson, Garth Fagan, Phyllis Lamhut, Anna Sokolow, and Donald McKayle—have kept the company from becoming a dance museum. But a healthy sprinkling of classics by Limón and modern dance pioneer Doris Humphrey, company artistic director until her death in 1958, provide impeccable ties to the roots of modernism.

The Limón Company has an impressive history, just like its founder. Born into a musical family in Mexico and raised in Arizona, Limón abandoned plans to be an artist after seeing a dance concert by the German expressionists Harold Kreutzberg and Yvonne Georgi. "I saw dance as a vision of ineffable power," he said, and promptly became a student of Humphrey and Charles Weidman. After an army stint during World War II, he formed his company in 1946. A master of dramatic dance set to lush scores, Limón created 74 works, among them *The Moor's Pavane* and *There Is a Time*. The troupe performs regularly at City Center and the Joyce Theater.

LAR LUBOVITCH DANCE COMPANY

15 W. 18th St.; (212) 242-0633

In more than 25 years as a choreographer, Lar Lubovitch has effort-lessly blurred stylistic barriers, creating technically intricate contempo-rary works performed as readily by top ballet companies and Broadway dancers as by his own outstanding modern dance troupe. Lubovitch's dances are musical with a sophisticated formal structure and hints of modern dance technique, notably José Limón-style weight changes. Typical is *A Brahms Symphony*, created for his company in 1985 and expanded for American Ballet Theater in 1995. The dance, performed by seven couples, is a lush, romantic whirlpool of patterns, built to the ebb and flow of Brahms's familiar Third Symphony. Taking his cue from the music, Lubovitch has also created pared down works to more minimal scores by Philip Glass and Steve Reich. "Of course the music comes first," he says.

MICHAEL MAO DANCE
215 W. 76th St.; (212) 595-5851

Michael Mao was born in Shanghai, studied ballet with David Howard and at the Joffrey School, and trained in modern dance at the Martha Graham school and Merce Cunningham studio. All of these influences inform the spare, abstract dances he makes for his 12-member ensemble (Mao enjoys working with large groups). His scores tend to be classical, and for a recent season at Kaye Playhouse, he choreographed new works to Beethoven's Piano Sonata #14 and Mahler's *Das Lied von der Erde*.

FIONA MARCOTTY DANCES
(212) 929-6804

Experimental choreographer Fiona Marcotty began her dance/choreography career in Boston and moved to New York in 1989. Since then she has performed her soft-edged, carefully constructed pieces, including her trademark solo *Watershed*, at the Kitchen and St. Mark's Church. Marcotty's key influences—classical sculpture, MTV videos, and Isadora Duncan—turn up in *Watershed*, in which she's eloquently partnered by a vast piece of blood-red velvet.

SUSAN MARSHALL & COMPANY

Susan Marshall, who began her company in 1983, favors vernacular movements over the codified vocabulary of ballet. Her experimental dances are built on walks, runs, falls, embraces, and other everyday moves, but the final results can be complex. Marshall's much-talked–about *Spectators at an Event* unfolded against a backdrop of huge images shot by the 1940s tabloid photographer WeeGee. The dances, performed by eight company members and a cast of 36 commmunity "volunteers," were interrupted periodically when the photographs would crash to the ground, a reminder of the randomness of castrophic events. The company has performed at BAM and Dance Theater Workshop. Marshall has also created works for the Frankfurt Ballet and Lyon Opera Ballet.

BEBE MILLER COMPANY
54 W. 21st St.; (212) 242-6433
"I'm trying to find a mix between the passion and pleasure of old dancing and the need to communicate," says dancer/choreographer Bebe Miller. So far, she's managed quite nicely. A native New Yorker, Miller danced with Dana Reitz and the Nina Wiener Dancers before starting her troupe in 1984. Since then, she has created more than 30 evocative abstract works, collaborating with a variety of composers, visual artists, and lighting designers. Her hard-edged, often frenzied dances range from solos to ensemble pieces. Her new *Tiny Sisters*, for six dancers, was inspired in part by the "Silent Twins," the true account of two West Indian sisters in England who created their own language and closed off the rest of the world. Miller's troupe has danced at Playhouse 91 and the Joyce Theater.

JOAN MILLER'S DANCE PLAYERS

(212) 568-8854

Founded in 1970, Joan Miller's Dance Players is one of the few companies based in the Bronx. Miller, who developed and directs the dance department at Lehman College, her troupe's home base, is known for her street smart, multimedia dance/theater pieces, which often address social issues. Sociopolitical satire is her specialty, although her dances occasionally are simply lyrical. Her troupe celebrated its twenty–fifth anniversary with a season at Florence Gould Hall.

ELISA MONTE DANCE

(212) 251-0789

"I was always obsessed with dance," says Elisa Monte, who performed with the Martha Graham Company, Lar Lubovitch, and Pilobolus, among others. Since creating her first work, *Treading*, in 1979, her obsession has taken form in intense, daring dances with an underlying energy and athleticism. Founded in 1981, her company won first prize at the International Dance Festival in Paris the following year. Since then, the troupe has performed internationally, and in New York at BAM, among other places. Monte likes collaborating with composers as well as artists—the sculptors Marisol and Louise Nevelson have both worked with her. In addition, the company dances works choreographed by co-founder David Brown, a Jamaican-born dancer who performed with the Martha Graham company.

MARK MORRIS DANCE GROUP

225 Lafayette St.; (212) 219-3660

Mark Morris's restlessly inventive dances are in the reps of countless dance companies, ballet and modern alike, from American Ballet Theater to the White Oak Dance Project, which Morris and Mikhail Baryshnikov co-founded in 1990. But Morris's own funky troupe is his foremost showcase. Musicality, humor, and a touching human beauty are at the root of Morris's dances, which veer from lighthearted to intense, often in the same piece. Music is never an afterthought but rather what determines the work's structure and feel, even in campy novelties like *The Hard Nut*, his yuletime send-up of *The Nutcracker*. Born in Seattle, Morris demanded dance lessons at age eight after seeing a performance of flamenco dancer José Greco. Ballet lessons followed, and at 19, Morris headed for New York, where he danced with almost everyone, it seems, including Eliot Feld, Laura Dean, Lar Lubovitch, and Hannah Kahn. His own troupe, formed in 1980 when he was 24, quickly attracted attention for Morris's audacious, free-wheeling choreography and equally freewheeling, gender-bending dancing. Eight years later, he replaced Maurice Bejart as Director of Dance at the Theatre Royal de la Monnaie in Brussels, where his company and his choreography mystified Belgians for three years. New York has proved a better fit, and his company regularly sells out at places like BAM and Lincoln Center.

JENNIFER MULLER/THE WORKS

131 W. 24th St.; (212) 691-3803

In 1995, Jennifer Muller/The Works celebrated its thirtieth season at the Joyce Theater with a look back at Muller's diverse, highly theatrical dances. Muller even brought back some of her former dancers to perform signature works like *Speed*, from 1974, "a jazzy, boisterous romp," as critic Jennifer Dunning put it. With a strong modern dance background—Muller performed with Pearl Lang, José Limón, and Louis Falco—she creates intense, physical dances, dramatically staged. An avid collaborator, she's worked with artists like Sandro Chia, Keith Haring, and Yoko Ono. She also sprinkles text into her dances. In *The Spotted Owl*, a plea to save the arts in America, dancers recite the words of Vance Packard and Vice-President Al Gore, among others.

YVES MUSARD & VADANCERS

In recent years, Yves Musard has developed site-specific works for public spaces, and at present, he's wending his way up Broadway in a continuing work called *The Broadway Project*. For the piece's first sector in 1994, he focused on the section of Broadway from Bowling Green to Times Square. More recently he turned his attention to the area from 168th Street to 215th Street. Mussard deals with elements of space, movement, and time, dissecting and paring down each movement. The result is "somehow akin to t'ai chi," as critic Anne Tobias put it.

NEO LABOS

Dance and performance are the twin hallmarks of Neo Labos, a company formed in 1989 to allow new artists to explore the edges of dance and theater. The company's two artistic directors, Michele Elliman and John O'Malley, have backgrounds in dance, choreography, video, and film. Elliman danced with the Eleo Pomare Dance Company and David Dorfman; O'Malley performed with the Dallas Ballet and Eglevsky Ballet. Their plotless pieces, often dealing with unruly passions, include collaborations with composers, artists, designers, and writers. *First Ascent*, a recent solo for Elliman, was based on Sally Mann's provocative photographs of adolescent girls on the brink of womanhood. Look for the company at SoHo's Ohio Theater.

PHOEBE NEVILLE DANCE COMPANY
(212) 393-9422

Phoebe Neville is an inspired minimalist, able to impart ecstasy, fear, or melancholy with a minimum of movement. A choreographer since the early 1960s, and head of her company since 1975, Neville makes works that explore the ways emotional energy is translated into movement. The results can be mysterious and evocative, as in *Prelude*, set to music by Olivier Messiaen, in which Neville lies on her back on the floor, her head to the audience and slowly raises, curves, then drops her arms. Period. Her company has performed at St. Mark's Church, Dance Theater Workshop, and Jacob's Pillow.

NIKOLAIS AND MURRAY LOUIS DANCE COMPANY
375 West Broadway; (212) 226-7700

In 1989, dancer/choreographer Murray Louis and veteran choreographer Alwin Nikolais merged their companies into a ten-member troupe that performs works by both men. The equation changed a bit in 1993 with the death of Nikolais at age 82. But Nikolais, whose highly theatrical, experimental dances blazed the way for multimedia performance, left over 100 works. Louis, known for witty, perceptive choreography with a huge artistic range, also has made more than 100 dances, including *Alone*, a moving 1994 tribute to his long-time companion and artistic collaborator. These days, the company is the resident troupe of the Kaye Playhouse.

Born in Connecticut, Nikolais started his career as an organist accompanying silent films. He switched to dance after seeing a performance by the great German modern dancer Mary Wigman, and in 1940 created his first work. Eight years later, he formed his company, creating controversial abstract dances, marked by bizarre costumes, strange gestures, electronic music, and weird lighting. Louis, a Brooklyn native, met Nikolais at a Colorado College summer session conducted by Hanya Holm. In 1949, he became lead soloist for the Nikolais troupe, where he performed for 20 years. He also formed his own company in 1953, and flexed his creative muscles during the 1980s dancing with the Dave Brubeck Jazz quartet and choreographing an evening-length program for Rudolf Nureyev.

TERE O'CONNOR DANCE

With works that combine intensity and obscurity, as one critic put it, Tere O'Connor has established himself as an experimental choreographer who creates dances displaying emotion and wit. After dancing with Rosalind Newman and Matthew Diamond, he began creating solos for himself and organized his own company in 1986, specializing in evening-length pieces. He also has choreographed commissioned solos for a variety of dancers, including Paola Rampone, which entailed a collaboration with composer David Linton and painter Sandro Chia. His company has performed at St. Mark's Church, the Kitchen, and Dance Theater Workshop.

PARSONS DANCE COMPANY

130 W. 56th St.; (212) 247-3203

"I like the knotted, squiggly stuff," dancer/choreographer David Parsons told an interviewer a while back. And his sharp, witty, often whimsical choreography includes all the above. Born in Illinois and raised in Kansas City, Missouri, Parsons headed for New York after high school with a scholarship to the Ailey School. But after seeing the Paul Taylor company, he talked his way into becoming an unofficial understudy. He finally made it onstage in 1978, when a dancer was injured during Taylor's Russian tour. Parsons quickly became a star, known for generously scaled moves and contrasts between speed and slowness. Such characteristics appear in his choreography. In 1987, Parsons, at 27, formed his own nine-member troupe, which tours extensively and has regular New York seasons at the Joyce Theater. He's still best known for *Caught,* his 1982, six-minute, crowd-pleasing solo with strobe-lit, mid-air freezes like photographic images; his more recent work has lost a bit of the earlier slickness and gimmickry, which has the critics cheering. (The audiences have cheered all along.)

PERIDANCE ENSEMBLE
132 Fourth Ave.; (212) 505-0886
Born in Israel, Igal Perry danced with Karmon, the Folk Dance Company of Israel, and studied classical ballet and the Graham technique before joining Bat-Dor Dance Company in 1968. So it's no surprise that his musical, high-energy choreography blends elements of ballet and modern dance. After a stint in the U.S. as choreographer and ballet master for Dennis Wayne's Dancers, he formed his 11-member company in 1984, a year after opening a large Greenwich Village school and studio. Perry's dancers have strong backgrounds in ballet and modern dance; current members danced with the Joffrey Ballet, Bolshoi Ballet, and Stephen Petronio. For a recent season at Kaye Playhouse, Perry choreographed to music by Bach, Chopin, Debussy, and Leonard Cohen.

STEPHEN PETRONIO COMPANY
95 St. Mark's Place; (212) 473-1660
No one could ever accuse Stephen Petronio of wasting time. He began dancing in 1974 while a student at Hampshire College and presented his first works that year. He formed his company in 1984, and along the way became one of the Trisha Brown Company's most distinctive dancers. These days, this Newark native devotes his time to choreographing for his nine-member troupe, inventing timely abstract pieces

known for extreme physical moves and pinpoint clarity. He seeks out intriguing collaborations with musicians (Yoko Ono, David Linton, the British post-punk band, Wire), fashion designers, and visual artists. *Surrender II*, a powerful 1989 duet for two men to a pulsating Linton score, features the muscular partners lifting, resisting, and yielding to each other. The troupe has danced at the Kitchen and the Joyce Theater.

ELEO POMARE DANCE COMPANY
325 W. 16th St.; (212) 924-4628

As artistic director of his own modern dance company for over 35 years, Eleo Pomare's impressive career is still flourishing. His seething 1962 classic about Harlem life, *Blues for the Jungle*, is still danced regularly throughout the country. And Pomare continues to make dances for his company, which most recently performed at Florence Gould Hall. Pomare's vivid, loosely narrative dances have touched upon social issues ranging from drug addition and poverty to aging. *A Horse Named Dancer*, a film about racehorses, serves as a backdrop for his performers, who, like horses, will eventually be retired by old age.

CLAIRE PORTER

A solo performer, Claire Porter melds movement and text into humorous, deadpan dance/performance pieces, called Portables, based on everyday events. *Fitness Digest*, in which Porter does nothing but sit on a stool, portrays a fitness instructor who issues commands to her imaginary class, clearly locked in her own mad world. Born in Connecticut, Porter was a computer programmer before focusing on dance (a performance by Maria Tallchief inspired the career change). After a stint studying dance at Ohio State, where she directed a dance company, she switched to solos. In New York she has performed at St. Mark's Church, PS 122, and Dia Performance Space.

PETER PUCCI PLUS DANCERS

Peter Pucci started his career with Pilobolus, where he spent nine years as a principal dancer, co-choreographer, and rehearsal director. It was strong training, and in 1986, he struck out on his own with Peter Pucci Plus Dancers. The Pilobolus influence pops up in Pucci's fondness for witty gymnastics and architectural choreography. A high point, literally, of *Moon of the Falling Leaves*, a tribute to Native Americans, comes when his all-male dancers do handstands and lock their legs together, creating a teepee form. Pucci's work is also known for intensity and playfulness. Besides appearances with his company at the Joyce Theater, Pucci has guested with the Joffrey Ballet, who dance his *Willing and Able*, the closing section of their evening-length Prince tribute, *Billboards*.

DANA REITZ

Based in Vermont, Dana Reitz makes regular forays to New York, performing at places like the Kitchen and in BAM's Next Wave Festival. Her works are usually danced in silence, which she believes emphasizes the musicality of the moves. Instead of musicians, she collaborates with lighting artists, notably Jennifer Tipton. A recent Kitchen performance with former Twyla Tharp dancer Sarah Rudner was a huge critical hit. After seeing it, Mikhail Baryshnikov commissioned a solo, *Uncharted Territory*, for his White Oak Dance Company.

PASCAL RIOULT DANCE THEATER

Many dance aficionados know Pascal Rioult as the striking Frenchman who danced with the Martha Graham Company in the mid-to-late 1980s (Graham showcased him in her last, unfinished work, *Eyes of the Goddess*). But Rioult began choreographing in 1989 and launched his six-dancer troupe in 1991, producing concerts at the Theater of

Riverside Church and Kaye Playhouse. Rioult, a top teenage hurdler in his native France, creates sharp, sentimentality-free works that tackle big subjects—*Harvest*, about human suffering, was inspired by Jean-François Millet's paintings of toiling farmers. Musically, he tends towards the classics, notably Ravel's *La Valse* and Arvo Pärt's *Te Deum*.

DAVID ROUSSEVE/REALITY

Choreographer David Rousseve danced in the companies of Jean Erdman, Kathryn Posin, Senta Driver, and the Toronto Dance Theater, among others. But he is also a writer, director, and actor, and his expressive multimedia works deftly meld theater and dance. Rousseve blends original music, mime, storytelling, and dance with African American culture to address a wide range of social topics, from racism and sexism to loss due to AIDS. At their best, evening–length works like *Urban Scenes/Creole Dreams*, with its complex, nonlinear narrative, live gospel choir, and story tracing three generations back to their Creole grandmother, can be dynamic, emotionally shattering, and highly original. Reality has performed in New York at BAM and Lincoln Center's Serious Fun festival.

LYNN SHAPIRO DANCE COMPANY

In a review of *Ambition Bird*, a 1994 work by Lynn Shapiro, critic Jennifer Dunning dubbed Shapiro the Francis Bacon of contemporary choreographers, creating a world "filled with bodies contorted and cramped by unexpressed feelings." Shapiro's dark choreography with its abstract, often nightmarish content, has gained attention in the last year or so, following performances organized by Dance Theater Workshop and Danspace. Born in Cambridge, Massachusetts—and a certified teacher of the Alexander Technique—Shapiro regularly collaborates with composers and presents her dances to live music.

TON SIMONS AND DANCERS

184 E. 3rd St.; (212) 460-9136

Dutch-born dancer/choreographer Ton Simons divides his time between his New York company, which performs at places like St. Mark's Church and Cunningham Studio, and the Rotterdam Dance Company, where he has been resident choreographer since 1987. Simons's dances are known for extremes of speed, dynamics, and complexity "balanced against moments of utter serenity and simplicity," as one critic put it. Juxtapositions and fragments fascinate him. In *Q*, danced to original music by Elliott Sharp, Simons created a series of duets and solos, then fragmented and spliced them together in changing combinations. The piece's three-sentence text by Simons was also fragmented and spliced in recitation by four performers.

ANNA SOKOLOW'S PLAYER'S PROJECT

c/o Lorry May, 543 Broadway; (212) 966-5621

In February of 1995, Anna Sokolow celebrated her 85th birthday with an enormous gala that attracted dance world luminaries Jerome Robbins, Paul Taylor, and Gerald Arpino. Small surprise. During nearly seven decades in modern dance, Sokolow's influence has been profound. After dancing with Martha Graham, she became a choreographer known for uncompromising dances protesting war and social evils. Her dances influenced an array of artists, from Taylor and Twyla Tharp to Alvin Ailey and Pina Bausch. She also choreographed for Broadway musicals, among them *Candide* and *Hair*. These days, Sokolow still creates dances for her Player's Project, which has kept much of her vast repertory alive. In a recent performance at Playhouse 91, the company danced *Dreams*, Sokolow's famous commentary on the Holocaust and the much lighter *September Sonnet*, a new—and, for Sokolow, angst-and-agony-free—love duet.

THE SOLOMONS COMPANY/DANCE

(212) 477-1321

Critics often use terms like brainy and cerebral to describe the choreography of dancer Gus Solomons jr. But the category it most consistently falls into is experimental. In *G. . . . Minor,* a recent solo piece set to music by J.S. Bach, Solomons, dressed in black pointe shoes and a red velvet robe that had belonged to choreographer Agnes de Mille, spent the entire dance seated majestically in a chair. Like his choreography, Solomons's background is unconventional. With an architecture degree from Massachusetts Institute of Technology, he zeroed in on dance, appearing with Martha Graham, Merce Cunningham, and Joyce Trisler. His own company came together in 1972 and has performed at Cunningham Studio and Lincoln Center's Serious Fun festival. Solomons also doubles as a dance reviewer, critiquing fellow choreographers and dancers in the *Village Voice* and *Dance Magazine*.

SOUNDANCE REPERTORY COMPANY

385 Broadway; (212) 941-6457

Formed in 1988, this ten-member contemporary company dances new works by five fledgling choreographers—Sean Curran, Heidi Latski, Lonne Moretton, Chris DC Ramos, and artistic director Sandra Stratton-Gonzalez. Their athletic, movement-rich dances are diverse. Stratton-Gonzalez makes theatrical, issue-oriented dances; Curran and Latski were influenced by their years dancing with choreographer Bill T. Jones. Besides productions by Dance Theater Workshop, the company performs in its small, mirrored studio.

SPOKE THE HUB DANCING
748 Union St., Brooklyn; (718) 857-5158
Begun in 1979 and currently one of Brooklyn's foremost arts organizations, Spoke the Hub Dancing also has a performance group, which has staged over 75 of founder Elise Long's dance/theater pieces, featuring casts of one to 100, with performers ranging in age from six months to 86 years. Besides appearances in informal settings like parades, pizza parlors, and parks, the group has performed at BAM.

ROSEANNE SPRADLIN
(212) 566-8041
Since moving to New York from Oklahoma in 1983, Roseanne Spradlin has created thoughtful, intensely performed abstract dances based on simple human movements. With a strong visual arts background, she often incorporated photographs into her work and is interested in depth of field. Besides recent performances at the Kitchen, she dances at SQUID, a performance space she helped start in 1994.

PAUL TAYLOR DANCE COMPANY
552 Broadway; (212) 431-5562
Critic Don McDonagh once described Paul Taylor's choreography as "a beautiful blend of athletic energy and humor which frequently occupies the ambiguous middle ground between tragedy and comedy." It's a near perfect description of Taylor's diverse, inventive dances. From *Epic*, a groundbreaking 1957 solo set to recorded telephone time signals, to the delightful *Company B*, a poignant 1993 romp set to Andrews Sisters'

songs, Taylor's work has been fresh, athletic, unpredictable, and in demand (more than 20 companies have produced it, including American Ballet Theater and the Houston Ballet). Born in Pennsylvania and raised in Washington, D.C., Taylor was a painter and swimmer before he discovered dance. But his natural ability landed him stints with Pearl Lang, Merce Cunningham, and, eventually, Martha Graham, where he was a star soloist from 1955 to 1962. Even George Balanchine recruited him for New York City Ballet's sleek *Episodes*. Taylor made his first dances in the mid 1950s and formed his company in 1961, where he performed until 1974. Long known for its superb dancers, Taylor's company, which camps out annually at City Center, has also nurtured a contingent of top choreographers, notably Twyla Tharp, David Parsons, and Victoria Uris.

URBAN BUSH WOMEN
225 Lafayette St.; (212) 343-0041
In just over a decade, artistic director Jawole Willa Jo Zollar has created a distinctive set of dances—and an equally distinctive identity—for Urban Bush Women, her black, all-female company. Highly theatrical, with live music and often a capella vocalizations, her works touch political aspects of pop culture. Topics can be raw—*Shelter*, an unsentimental look at homelessness, has been performed by the Alvin Ailey Dance Theater as well as her own troupe. Some themes are pleasingly frivolous—*Girlfriends* centers on a slumber party. In New York, look for Urban Bush Women at places like PS 122 and the Joyce Theater.

DOUG VARONE AND DANCERS
(212) 966-0861
Doug Varone spent the early part of his career dancing with the José Limón Dance Company and, eventually Lar Lubovitch, where he also

taught. Since 1986, when he formed his eight-member troupe, his athletic, highly musical dances have won strong reviews. With no obvious narrative, Varone's dances express emotion through movement that's powerful and often raw. His musical tastes are wide-ranging, everything from Schubert to contemporary stalwarts like John Adams and Philip Glass. Varone also does guest choreography. He's made ice dances for Brian Orser and Paul and Isabelle Duchesnay. And he choreographed designer Geoffrey Beene's Spring '95 fashion show, in which models *and* dancers wore the clothes.

WHITE OAK DANCE PROJECT

To date, Mikhail Baryshnikov's White Oak Dance Project, begun in 1990, has performed only once in New York. But its weeklong 1994 season at New York State Theater sold out and the company often uses Manhattan practice studios. Most of Baryshnikov's dancers are New Yorkers as well, notably older dancers whose age and maturity he considers assets. Unlike modern companies that present the work of one choreographer, White Oak's expanding repertory includes many styles by numerous dance makers, from Merce Cunningham to Twyla Tharp. Baryshnikov's star power is the company's obvious attraction, for dance sophisticates and neophytes alike—prior to a recent appearance at Jacob's Pillow, the box office reported callers requesting tickets for "Mikhail Gorbachev's dance company." But White Oak offers plenty besides one of the greatest dancers in the world.

THE KEVIN WYNN COLLECTION

Since his company's inception in 1981, dance enthusiasts, including numerous fledgling dancers, have flocked to Wynn's energetic, movement-filled pieces. A former soloist with the José Limón Dance Company, Wynn worked with Jowale Willa Jo Zollar of Urban Bush

Woman and Daniel Nagrin. In *Of Sushi, Collard Greens and Salsa*, performed at the Bessie Schönberg Theater, 14 superb dancers clad in black lift, manipulate and pivot one another against a background of political speeches about violence and prejudice. Wynn's company is set to perform at the Joyce Theater's *Altogether Different* festival in January 1996.

BILL YOUNG & DANCERS
Even in still photographs, Bill Young's handsome dance troupe looks intensely physical. There are lifts galore—a woman, feet pointed sharply, balances on a man's back, and a man, head shaved, is held high by another so their bodies create a right angle. In performance, these often sensual movements occur at a rapid pace and, though abstract, can tap a variety of emotions. In *Interleaving*, from 1987, Young created four separate dances, then grouped the four beginnings together, followed by the four middles and the quartet of endings. Born in Durham, N.C., Young began making dances in 1979 as a member of the Margaret Jenkins Dance Company in San Francisco. His current company, formed in 1986, has danced at the Joyce Theater, the Kitchen, and PS 122.

∼ BALLROOM, JAZZ, TAP AND ∼ HIP-HOP COMPANIES

AMERICAN BALLROOM THEATER
129 W. 27th St.; 212) 627-8337
This is the ultimate company for anyone who has ever watched a ballroom dance competition and wondered what the top contestants could do if allowed to simply dance—without a number on their backs or the constricted moves dictated by the competition rules. This stylish

company presents shimmering waltzes, foxtrots, tangos, sambas, cha chas, and other standards in a concert setting. Dances are specially choreographed by veterans of ballet, jazz, and Broadway like Geoffrey Holder, Gary Piercen, and Peter Anastos—and presented by an international collection of dancers fluent in ballet, modern, and jazz. All, including artistic directors Pierre Dulaine and Yvonne Marceau, have competed professionally—and successfully. In New York look for their annual two-week season at the Joyce Theater, complete with marabou feathers and silver slippers.

AMERICAN TAP DANCE ORCHESTRA
170 Mercer St.; (212) 925-3980

The American Tap Dance Orchestra is precisely what its name promises: the dancers' feet become instruments to create a range of musical tones and rhythms. It's a symphony of sole with additional music by live jazz musicians and vocalists. Formed in 1986 by Brenda Bufalino, one of rhythm tap's preeminent dancers and choreographers, the company has set the standard for tap troupes and has danced all over the world, with local stints at the Joyce Theater, Town Hall, and Kaye Playhouse. Guest artists have included Gregory Hines and Charles "Honi" Coles. But for the most part, audiences see the company's core dancers, clad in spiffy black suits, white shirts, and those magical, musical shoes.

GHETTORIGINAL
(212) 505-0886

Hip-hop artists are usually seen on MTV or on the street, but Ghett-Original's 12 dancers perform on concert stages at places like Kennedy Center and PS 122. Formed a few years ago, the group brought together Hispanic and African American members of pioneering hip-hop groups, such as Magnificent Force, Rhythm Technicians, and Rock

Steady Crew—and Masami Kanemoto, from Tokyo, where hip-hop is wildly popular. The choreography blends elements of breakdancing, tap, jazz dance, African dance, and capoeira, all presented with an intense physicality.

JAZZ DANCE AMERICA

This is a new company, formed in 1992 by dancer/choreographer Maurice Brandon Curry. But already it has accomplished much of what Curry, who has choreographed videos for Prince, set out to do. The troupe performs nothing but jazz dance, which Curry defines as an amalgam of tap, modern, and contemporary social dancing, from disco to funk. A recent performance at the Pace Downtown Theater featured contemporary and jazz dances, including a re-creation of the jazz ballet classic *Slaughter on Tenth Avenue*, choreographed in 1948 by Gene Kelly. Guest dancers have included ABT's Ashley Tuttle and Charles Askegard.

JAZZDANCE BY DANNY BURACZESKI

Though jazz choreographer Danny Buraczeski is now based in Minneapolis/St. Paul, he danced for years in New York and his nine-member company appears fairly regularly at the Joyce Theater. A performer for over 20 years, Buraczeski specializes in dances set to jazz rhythms—music that swings. Burazceski makes concert dances; the dancers relate to one another on stage instead of coming at the audience, pelvises a-jiggle. His musical palette is broad, with dances set to works by Dave Brubeck, Thelonious Monk, Artie Shaw, and Tito Puente, among others.

KNICKS CITY DANCERS

New York Knicks, 2 Pennsylvania Plaza; (212) 465-6118

Purists would never call the Knicks City Dancers jazz dancers, but their sassy amalgam of hip-hop, MTV moves, and aerobics-class bumps and grinds is urban and slick, exactly what you'd expect at a pro basketball game. Voluminous Sarah Jessica Parker hair seems as much a prerequisite as a strong jump and sashaying skills. By far the best dance team in the NBA's Eastern Division, the City Dancers are close competition for the Western Division's famed Laker Girls.

MANHATTAN TAP

(212) 674-1572

Sound is a big part of the aesthetic for Manhattan Tap, Heather Cornell's six-member rhythm tap company. In one seven-minute dance, the taps literally *are* the music. Cornell, a polished tap dancer and choreographer, believes tap and jazz music are intertwined; as proof, her company performs to live jazz, much of its scored expressly for the troupe. The dances deftly blend improvisation and choreography. Since its debut in 1986, the company has appeared at places like Kaye Playhouse and the Village Gate jazz club, frequently accompanied by guest tap masters like Gregory Hines and "Buster" Brown.

MICKEY D. & FRIENDS

209 E. 5th St.; (212) 477-6372

Dancer/choreographer Mickey Davidson formed her company of dancers, singers, and musicians in 1982 to explore the relationship between dance and music, particularly African and African American music. The company quickly developed a wide-ranging repertory of dance styles, including African, Lester Horton-style modern dance, and, of course, tap, sand and jazz dances, from Lindy hop to rap.

Davidson also created choreography for the twentieth-anniversary production of writer Ntozake Shange's *For Colored Girls*. She and her troupe have danced at Context Studios and Greenwich House.

RADIO CITY MUSIC HALL ROCKETTES

1260 Avenue of the Americas; (212) 632-4000

More than almost any other dance troupe, the Rockettes are a New York City institution, like the Brooklyn Bridge or, well, Rockefeller Center. In fact, they spend much of their time on the road, in distinctly un-New Yorkish places like Branson, Missouri, and Las Vegas. But always, they head home to show off their slick, precision kicks and syncronized Broadway-style tapping at Radio City's annual Christmas spectacular, Easter show, and Macy's Thanksgiving's Day parade. Competition to join the classic 32-member line is tough, open to dancers from 5 feet 5 1/2–9 inches tall. They're expected to know ballet, tap, jazz, and modern dance *and* be able to sing. Since 1932, when the Rockettes debuted at Radio City on opening night, the cumulative Rockette sorority has soared past 2,000 members.

SILVER BELLES

(212) 316-4162

In the 1930s and 1940s, no performance at Harlem's Apollo Theater was complete without the club's chorus line, a glamorous ensemble of 16 exceptional tappers who easily challenged the Rockettes for legginess and virtuosity and who often appeared with big–band greats like Duke Ellington and Count Basie. In 1986, six of these veterans dusted off their tap shoes and formed the Silver Belles. "I'm old, but I'm not cold," explained company choreographer Bertye Lou Wood. Members range in age from 65 to over 80. Dressed in their signature satin trousers, they've danced at music, tap, and charity functions throughout the New York area, including at Alice Tully Hall and the Atlantis Casino in Atlantic City.

TAP EXPRESS
258 W. 15th St.; (212) 691-8972

In 1994, dancer/choreographer Robin Tribble left American Tap Dance Orchestra to form her own company, Tap Express. Since then, her rhythm tap company — ten dancers tapping to live music—has danced at the Hudson Guild Theater, among other New York haunts. Tribble believes tap is a form of music. That music is accompanied mainly by jazz — classic bop, swing and Latin jazz. Tribble's choreographic goal is to push the boundaries of tap, which she studied with Charles "Cookie" Cook, Chuck Green, and Brenda Bufalino.

TEN TOE PERCUSSION ENSEMBLE/IRA BERNSTEIN
(516) 593-6419

Rhythm tap is a specialty of Ira Bernstein, who dances as a solo performer and with his stepdance group, the Ten Toe Percussion Ensemble. He also performs ethnic strains of percussive dance—Appalachian flatfoot clogging, English clogging, Irish stepdancing, and South African boot dancing. The rep means a wardrobe of footwear, from tap shoes to wooden clogs, and a willingness to tap his toes to everything from live jazz to folk fiddles. "I'm the drummer," he says, calling his feet the sticks and the floor the drum. A former member of the American Tap Dance Orchestra, he's performed at Symphony Space and Town Hall.

~ ETHNIC DANCE GROUPS ~

AMERICAN SPANISH DANCE THEATER/ANDREA DEL CONTE
(212) 674-6725

Andrea Del Conte's annual winter season at the Thalia Spanish Theater in Sunnyside, Queens is a high point for flamenco enthusiasts. Del Conte and her three-member company, formed in 1979, perform traditional flamenco with a singer, two guitarists, and a percussion artist. Born in upstate New York, Del Conte studied Spanish classical and flamenco dance in Spain and still visits regularly to brush up her craft. Since 1975, she has appeared as a solo performer, dancing with other flamenco companies and the New York City Opera.

BALLET HISPANICO
167 W. 89th St.; (212) 362-6710

Widely considered the nation's foremost Hispanic American dance company, Ballet Hispanico is based on the West Side but travels widely. Formed in 1970 by artistic director Tina Ramirez, the company deftly blends ballet and modern dance with flamenco, classical Spanish, and traditional Caribbean dances. Not surprisingly, Ramirez cites three diverse choreographers—Anna Sokolow, Marachi Carmelita, and Bob Fosse—as her prime influences. The company repertory, including works by Talley Beatty, Graciela Daniele, and Vicente Nebrada, neatly reflects Ramirez's artistic background. Born in Venezuela to a Puerto Rican mother and Mexican bullfighter father, she was raised in New York, where she studied ballet with Alexandra Danilova, modern dance with Sokolow, and Spanish dance with Lola Bravo. Ramirez is serious about making Hispanic culture part of the troupe's esthetic. Though she frequently commissions works from experimental choreographers like Susan Marshall and Amanda Miller, they must use music associated with Spain or Latin America. The results can be delightful. In *Solo*, Marshall had dancer José Costa do a flamenco dance on a ramp while balancing a water-filled punch bowl on his head.

MARIA BENITEZ TEATRO FLAMENCO
(212) 689-9162

There's a terrific publicity picture of Maria Benitez; head raised, back arched, Benitez embodies flamenco to her fingertips. Small surprise she is one of the few American flamenco artists to gain acceptance from snobbish Spaniards, who maintain only natives truly understand flamenco. Based in New York and her native New Mexico, where she holds a flamenco workshop each summer, Benitez and her company specialize in new ways of presenting this increasingly adaptable dance. Besides traditional dance suites, the company does theatrical pieces. In *El Muro*, based on Federico Garcia Lorca's poem *The Gypsy Nun*, Benitez explores the nun's dreams of sensuality through flamenco. Look for the company at places like the Joyce Theater and Jacob's Pillow.

PAT CANNON FOOT & FIDDLE DANCE COMPANY
(718) 753-6950

It's hard to categorize Pat Cannon and her able company of soloists, but audiences often hoot and holler when they come on stage. The dancing veers from Appalachian clogging and 1940s jitterbugging, to Texas two-step and sand dancing that's pure vaudeville. What links these diverse dance styles is their American roots; Cannon tosses in show dance elements as well. A tap dancer by training, Cannon performed with country-and-western singers early in her career and is an experienced folk dance caller. Along the way, she refined authentic folk material from the South and Southwest for the stage. The results have won her company regular stints at Playhouse 91 and Marymount Manhattan Theater.

DANCEBRAZIL

This vibrant company, under artistic director Jelon Vieira, performs original dances that blend traditional Afro-Brazilian dance with North American modern dance. At the root of Vieira's vigorous choreography is capoeria, a Brazilian strain of the martial arts originally from Angola and West Africa. Capoeria is particularly evident in Vieira's 1993 stylized evening-length dance, *Pivete*, based on Jorge Amado's 1937 novel *Capitaes da Areia*, about impoverished street urchins in Brazil's Bahia section. Vieira, born in Bahia, has lived and worked in the United States since 1975. He has choreographed for Broadway shows, movies, and, of course, his company, which has danced at BAM and St. Mark's Church.

FLAMENCO LATINO

250 W. 54th St.; (212) 399-8519

It seems only natural that as flamenco makes its way through America's Hispanic cultures, it melds with Latin America's distinctive dance rhythms. This blend of Spanish and Hispanic dance styles is precisely what Flamenco Latino offers. The company's five female performers, accompanied by drums, flute and flamenco guitar, present dances that set traditional flamenco heelwork to Latin rhythms like Puerto Rican Bomba and Dominican Merengue. Formed in 1979, this likeable company, founded by dancer/choreographer Aurora Reyes and her guitarist husband, Basilio Georges, has gained momentum in the last few seasons, performing at small theaters like the American Theater of Actors and clubs like Boca Chica.

DONNY GOLDEN

(718) 238-9207

Brooklyn native Donny Golden was the first American-born Irish step-dancer ever to win a medal in stepdance's two champagne events—the

All-Ireland and All-World senior men's championships in Dublin. Golden's competitive days are over, but his performing days are in full flow. He's a featured stepdancer with two internationally known Irish music companies, Cherish the Ladies and Green Fields of America. And he frequently performs with the Irish music group, the Chieftans. He also turns up locally at events sponsored by Dancing in the Streets and the Prospect Park Bandshell. Irish stepdancing, a precursor of tap, entails fancy footwork—swift, high kicks, clicking heels and other nimble moves—with the body held as still as possible. And interest is growing. "It used to be only in March," Golden says.

JAPAN SOCIETY

333 E. 47th St.; (212) 752-3015

Traditional and contemporary dance and theater groups from Japan perform several times a year on the Japan Society's handsome proscenium stage. The mix is almost equally divided between traditional performers in Noh, Kabuki, and mime and dancers specializing in everything from butoh, Japan's premiere avant-garde dance form, to contemporary dances that blend modern, postmodern, and butoh. Recent performers have included heartthrob Kabuki actor Bando Tamasaburo, an Okinawan dance troupe, butoh pioneer Kazuo Ono and New York's Eiko & Koma.

LA CONJA MIMBRE Y VARETA

(212) 541-4455

La Conja, a popular flamenco dancer and singer known for her appearances with José Greco, formed her own company in 1994. Since then her troupe, Mimbre y Vareta, has performed at Pace Downtown Theater. La Conja is one of the dancers breathing new life into flamenco. Her company—three lead dancers, a singer, and six musicians—qualifies as traditional, not stodgy. Live music is a big part of each performance; La Conja chose her company's name, branch and twigs, to symbolize the closeness of music and flamenco. Her dancing is known for its intensity, exquisitely controlled fireworks, and quiet experimentation.

CHARLES MOORE DANCE THEATER

379 Bridge St., Brooklyn; (718) 467-7127

Since company founder Charles Moore's death in 1985, his wife, Ella Thompson Moore, has kept both his school and his company alive. Both are dedicated to performing and teaching the history of black dance and music, from its roots in African ceremony to its evolution from plantation days to gospel sounds and swing at places like Harlem's Savoy Ballroom in the 1940s. The company showpiece is *Traces*, an evening-long piece that follows the development of African music and dance in this country. Besides the Moores, company choreographers have included Charles "Cookie" Cook and Pepsi Bethel.

NOCHE FLAMENCA

(212) 580-0094

Though based in Madrid, this seven-member flamenco company was begun by New Yorker Martin Santangelo and has frequent New York seasons, most recently at Theater 80 in St. Mark's Place. Noche Flamenca's notion of flamenco is purely Spanish, with no North American influences. Much of the work, accompanied by live singers and two guitarists, is improvised solos, like jazz. Santangelo, whose Argentinian mother was a dancer, started out as an actor with Teatro Campesino in California and discovered his calling when a character he portrayed danced flamenco. He went to Madrid to learn flamenco, danced for a while with Maria Benitez and eventually formed his own company with his wife, dancer Soledad Barrio.

PILAR RIOJA

Repertorio Espanol, 138 E. 27th St.; (212) 889-2850

Spanish dancer Pilar Rioja lives in Mexico, where she was born to Spanish parents. But for more than two decades, she has summered in New York, where loyal fans flock to her annual hot-weather performances at the intimate Gramercy Arts Theater. Rioja, who studied dance in Spain, stresses that she is a *Spanish* dancer, whose repertory includes but is not limited to flamenco. In a recent season, she performed a traditional Andalusian dance accompanied by castanets and piano and a stylized dance from the Bolero School, which mixes 17th-century ballet technique with Spanish folk elements. She also presented two flamenco dances with their formidable footwork. Though Rioja is a solo performer, she puts on a big show, accompanied by a singer, two guitarists, and a pianist.

ROOTS OF BRAZIL

(718) 622-1561

This sexy dance group, led by singer and artistic director Lygya Barreto, performs to live music with a heavy samba beat. A native of Rio de Janeiro, Barreto, dubbed the Brazilian folk-music answer to Paula Abdul by a New York critic, has a solid dance background; she's studied jazz, modern, and ballet at Alvin Ailey. The troupe, which dances to an amalgam of traditional Brazilian rhythms, pop, jazz, and samba, has appeared at Carnegie Hall and BAM and turns up frequently at clubs like the Ballroom, S.O.B.'s, and Birdland.

～ FOLK DANCE COMPANIES ～

BOSILEK BULGARIAN FOLK DANCE ENSEMBLE
(908) 828-2887

This New York-based, all-women troupe has performed Bulgarian folk dances since 1979 and presents half-hour shows regularly at festivals, churches, museums, and libraries. "Bulgarian dance is popular because it's rhythmic, says group leader Cathie Springer. "It's lively, involving lots of leg movements, with less leaping than Hungarian dance, less stomping than Transylvanian." Much of the dancing is done in a counterclockwise circle, with dancers holding hands. Though members are amateurs, many have studied and performed in Bulgaria and all dance in traditional Bulgarian costumes.

THE BOUWERIE BOYS MORRIS DANCERS
(914) 265-4273

Begun in Binghamton, New York, in 1979 by John Dexter, a violinist with the Manhattan String Quartet, the Bouwerie Boys specialize in Morris dances specifically from the village of Sherbourne in England's Cotswold region. Six-men groups, wearing white trousers and black jackets, dance to the music of the three-holed pipe, tabor, and melodeon. The five-to-ten-minute dances, full of vigorous jumping, leaping, and pre-medieval aerobics, create set formations, sandwiched between choruses. Morris dancing's rich history stretches into the mists of time. Though almost wiped out by the Industrial Revolution, Morris resurfaced in 1899 and flourishes today with nearly 200 groups in the U.S. alone. Prosperity, good luck, and fertility are supposed to come to all who watch. The Bouwerie Boys have a full dance card that includes Easter dances in Central Park and a 6:30 a.m. May Day maypole frolic in Riverside Park, 93rd Street entrance.

EUROPEAN FOLK FESTIVAL

Sponsored by the Slavic Council, this annual performance evening at Alice Tully Hall in January or February, gathers the cream of New York's amateur, and quasi-amateur, ethnic dance groups. Originally limited to the Slavics and Eastern Europeans, the festival recently expanded to embrace dances from all of Europe, including groups specializing in Norwegian dances and English and French sword dances.

HALF MOON SWORD
(212) 242-7131

Dance historians claim the sword dance was an early version of the Cotswold Morris dance, brought to England by Danes. Ancient sword dances, according to *Culture Heritage* magazine, were performed by six to eight men, linked together by three–foot–long swords. Once linked, the men danced elaborate figures and criss-crosses. But this is America, and one of the country's premiere sword-dancing groups is the women-only Half Moon Sword. The group performs old-style sword dances—"stately and mysterious," says company member Sarah Henry—with long swords of Sheffield steel and newer, zippier sword dances with short, flexible rapiers, which allow the linked dancers to negotiate more elaborate formations. The ten–member group holds a two-day sword dance festival on President's Day weekend, with performances at Sony Plaza and Penn Station, and a Sunday grand finale, usually at the picnic house in Brooklyn's Prospect Park.

LIMBORA SLOVAK FOLK ENSEMBLE
P.O. Box 143, Rockefeller Center, New York 10185;
(212) 557-1511

This active troupe, comprising ten couples and seven musicians, was the first Slovak-American folk dance group to tour what was once

Czechoslovakia. Back home, Limbora performs 15 to 20 times a year at street fairs like the Ninth Avenue Food Festival, Czech and Slovak festivals and picnics, and the European Folk Festival. Dances originate from all over Slovakia, where each village has its own dance steps *and* handmade costumes. (Troupe members need big closets.) Musicians play the accordian, violin, and bass, with occasional accompaniments on the clarinet and the cimbal, which is a large stringed instrument hit with wooden mallets. Dances—"very fast paced and uplifting," says director Milan Paul Spisek—reflect regional distinctions.

NEW SCOTLAND DANCERS
(212) 744-1470 (afternoons and evenings)
Started by a Scotsman who later returned to Dundee, the New Scotland Dancers perform mainly on weekends for church groups, at schools and rest homes, and for Scottish organizations like the St. Andrews Society. The group's four couples, a traditional "set," dance reels, jigs, and slow, elegant strathspeys, the women dressed in long white dresses with tartan sashes, the men in kilts and black velvet jackets. "The steps are not that intricate, but it's very disciplined," says longtime member Sheila Wilson.

NEW WORLD SWORD
(914) 835-6551
This all–men's sword–dancing group, lead by Stephen Corrsin, arguably the nation's premiere authority on sword and Morris dance, practices two to four times a month and performs throughout the New York area. While some sword–dancing groups use sword surrogates of metal or wood, New World's mighty men use actual swords and mainly perform dances from Austria and other parts of central Europe.

POLISH AMERICAN FOLK DANCE

(718) 389-1141

Begun in 1938—and rejuvinated in 1968—this proficient troupe of men and women stages lavish productions of Polish dance with live music. The company has toured and performed in Poland seven times, makes an annual appearance at the Harvest Festival at Callicoon Center, a Polish resort in the Catskills, and has danced regularly at Alice Tully Hall since 1970 (their next Tully visit is scheduled for 1996). "Polish music is extremely melodic," says Stanley Pelc, company president and director. "And the dances move in intricate formations with lots of movement to get you there."

RING O'BELLS

(212) 242-7131

The oldest women's Morris dance group in America, this 20-member team celebrated its twentieth anniversary in 1994. Like Bouwrie Boys, their athletic, jump-filled Morris dances hail from England's Cotswold region and display similar steps. But with dances specifically from the Oxfordshire village of Ascot-under-Wychwood, their precise presentations differ. Dressed in black knickerbockers, blue vests, and shirts festooned with ribbons and bells, the group dances in front of the Plaza Hotel during the Easter parade and turns up at street fairs, farmers markets, and, frequently, in Washington Square Park and the Brooklyn Heights Promenade.

SWEDISH FOLK DANCERS OF NEW YORK

(914) 725-3543

The oldest Swedish dance group in the land, this New York troupe demonstrates traditional Swedish line, circle, and couple dances at a variety of Swedish festivals along the East Coast, including the annual

Swedish Day Festival in New York. The group's eight couples perform in traditional Swedish costumes and hold dances for the public periodically at restaurants or halls.

TACHIBANA DANCE GROUP

(718) 327-8356

Tachibana, named for a pretty orange flower, is a prominent Tokyo dance school. This group, trained by Tachibana instructors from Japan, performs Japanese classical and folk dances. Classical dances resemble the elegant, studied dances of Kabuki. Folk dances are regional, with distinctive steps and music. Tachibana specializes in folk dances from Japan's northern Sugaru region, "known for livelier dances with a rhythm beat on a samisen," says Toyo Kikuchi, a group leader. Tachibana offers demonstrations at museums, schools, and festivals in the New York area.

TOMOV FOLK DANCE ENSEMBLE

Concert Artists Management, 59 W. 58th St.;
(212) 593-1640; (718) 639-3465

This polished, highly professional group of 40 dancers, singers and musicians performs dances from the regions that made up the former Yugoslavia—Croatia, Serbia, Macedonia, Bosnia, Slovenia and the unfixed areas where gypsies wander. The group's dynamic leader, George Tomov, danced professionally for years with Lado and Tanec, two prominent Yugoslav national dance ensembles, before moving to New York in 1968. These days he also teaches Balkan folk dance here and throughout the country. The troupe's repertory is huge and historical, bulging with dances marked by complex rhythms and steps; several are over 800 years old. Costumes are equally authentic, handmade and embroidered in the Balkans; an elaborate bride's gown from Macedonia is embedded with 17th-century jewelry. The group has performed at Carnegie Hall, Avery Fisher Hall, and Hunter College.

∼ COMPANIES THAT DANCE ON SKATES ∼

ICE THEATER OF NEW YORK
Sky Rink at Chelsea Piers, 23rd St. at Hudson River;
(212) 336-6100
Ice Theater of New York was formed in 1984 as something different— a company that promotes figure skating as a performing art rather than a competitive event or commercial entertainment. In short, no judges and no skating Snow Whites— just dancing on thin metal blades with steps shaped by modern dance choreographers such as Laura Dean, Ann Carlson, and William Whitener. Since its inception, the company has danced regularly at every major rink in town (check out their free noontime ice concerts at Rockefeller Plaza), and it has toured widely. The 18-member company regularly recruits well-known guests, like 1994 Olympic silver medalists Maia Usova and Alexandre Zhulin. Expect performances to become more frequent in the company's terrific new digs overlooking the water at Chelsea Piers.

NYC SKATE CREW
Roller Rinks at Chelsea Piers, 23rd St. at Hudson River;
(212) 336-6200
This professional in-line skate troupe, with four core bladers, perform up-to-the-minute hip-hop, funk, and fitness routines on wheels, choreographed to the latest music. While many of their moves are complex versions of what can be seen in funk aerobics classes, they also do jumps, lifts, and death spirals borrowed from competitive ice skating. Intricate ensemble maneuvers, using four or

more skaters at once, are a Skate Crew trademark. Founder and choreographer Diane Goldberg hails from Los Angeles' Team Roller Blade, the nation's first performing in-line skate troupe. But NYC Skate Crew also qualifies as a pioneer in the weird, wonderful world of professional in-line dancing.

∼ NEW JERSEY COMPANIES ∼

AMERICAN REPERTORY BALLET COMPANY

80 Albany St., New Brunswick; (908) 249-1254

The American Repertory Ballet Company, formed in 1978, built its reputation as the Princeton Ballet Company, performing arm of the Princeton Ballet School. The school and the renamed company, one of New Jersey's two leading ballet troupes, are still linked. And though the 1991 name change still irritates local purists, it reflects what the company dances as well as the troupe's less regional aspirations. The current repertory, under artistic director Septime Webre, features works like Alvin Ailey's *The Lark Ascending*, George Balanchine's *Rubies*, Webre's full-length *Romeo and Juliet* and, of course, *The Nutcracker*. The season, with residencies at McCarter Theatre in Princeton and the State Theatre in New Brunswick, runs from September through May, leaving plenty of touring time.

DENISHAWN REPERTORY DANCERS/
NJ CENTER DANCE COLLECTIVE

28 W. State St., Trenton; (609) 394-8074

Though based in Trenton, the Denishawn Repertory Dancers has had a strong New York City presence since its 1988 debut. The troupe, with top dancers from Martha Graham, Eleo Pomare, and Feld Ballets/NY, performs faithful reconstructions of dances by modern dance pioneers Ruth St. Denis (1879–1968), her husband, Ted Shawn (1891–1972), and Doris Humphrey (1895–1958). The troupe's New Jersey home is appropriate. St. Denis made her dancing debut at 14, in Somerville, before becoming the toast of Europe with her "oriental" dances. In 1915, she and Shawn founded the Denishawn Dancers and its school, where Martha Graham and Charles Weidman studied; the rest is modern dance history. Begun in 1981 by Michele Mathesius, who heads the dance division at New York's High School of Performing Arts, the company performs faithful Denishawn reconstructions shaped by artistic advisor Jane Sherman, a former Denishawn Dancer.

NAI-NI CHEN DANCE COMPANY

397 Lincoln Ave., Fort Lee; (201) 947-8403

Dancer/choreographer Nai-Ni Chen was born in Taiwan, and her delicate choreography blends elements of Western contemporary dance with the aesthetics and concepts of Chinese visual art. In Taiwan, Chen performed traditional Chinese opera technique and folk dance. In the U.S., where she arrived in 1982, she studied dance at New York University before forming her company in 1988. A recent work, *Calligraphy II*, was inspired by the elegant lines of motion made by the brush pen in Chinese caligraphy. Chen's company has performed at St. Mark's Church in Manhattan and the Wayne, N.J., YM/YWHA.

CAROLYN DORFMAN DANCE COMPANY

2780 Morris Ave., Union; (908) 687-8855

In *Dance/Stories, Part I*, a recent work by Carolyn Dorfman, the Union-based choreographer created an interdisciplinary piece that blended dance with a backdrop of folk tales narrated by storyteller Charlotte Blake Alston and original music by drummer/composer Horace Arnold and jazz violinist John Blake. Though ambitious, the piece was no departure. At the helm of her own eight-member troupe since 1982, Dorfman, an admirer of Doris Humphrey and José Limón, makes works that use weight and breathing as motivation for movement. Several Limón pieces are also in the rep.

NEW JERSEY BALLET COMPANY
270 Pleasant Valley Way, West Orange; (201) 736-5940
From its first performance at a Newark high school in 1958, New Jersey Ballet has grown into a leading regional company, with residencies at Paper Mill Playhouse in Millburn and Kean College in Union, international tours that have included Russia, Italy, and Taiwan and an impressive roster of 17 polished young performers. The talent is both onstage (the company's women are particularly strong) and backstage (besides *two* resident choreographers, artistic advisors include former American Ballet Theater principal Eleanor D'Antuono, New York City Ballet great Edward Villella, and Leonid Kozlov, formerly of NYCB and the Bolshoi). The rep, bulging with more than 70 works, includes sprinklings of Balanchine (*Allegro Brillante*), de Mille (*Rodeo*), and full-length productions of *Cinderella* and *The Nutcracker*.

NICHOLAS RODRIGUEZ & DANCE COMPASS
P.O. Box 43115, Upper Montclair; (201) 744-7420
A New Jersey native, Nicholas Rodriguez started his lively company of multicultural dancers in 1984 as a showcase for his contemporary choreography. Since then, the troupe has toured widely, performing at BAM, Dance Theater Workshop, and Jacob's Pillow as well as a variety of New Jersey venues, from Life Hall at Montclair State University to Kean College in Union. Rodriguez, a skilled performer, creates a varied

range of works that display psychological, emotional, and Latin influences, from pure movement to dances with plot and character.

∽ CONNECTICUT DANCE COMPANIES ∽

CONNECTICUT BALLET
20 Acosta St., Stamford; (203) 978-0771
The Connecticut Ballet started life in 1981 as Ballet Today at the Jacob's Pillow Dance Festival in upstate Massachusetts. But these days, the resident company of the Stamford Center for the Arts is a Connecticut institution. The 16-member company dances three brief seasons at the center—a winter *Nutcracker*, a spring full-length work, like *Giselle* or *Coppelia*, and a late-spring mixed bill of ballet, modern, and jazz. Besides artistic director Brett Raphael, who has choreographed one-act and full–length ballets, Ann Reinking, Joseph Locarro, and company co-founder Luk de Layress have choreographed for the troupe. Works by Anna Sokolow, Lynne Taylor-Corbett, and Danny Buraczeski round out the rep. The troupe regularly recruits guest dancers like Cynthia Gregory, Stephanie Saland, and Fernando Bujones. But Raphael has high hopes to soon feature graduates of the Connecticut Ballet Center, the company school.

HARTFORD BALLET
226 Farmington Ave.; (860) 525-9396
This polished, 19-member company, begun in 1972, dances a far-reaching repertory, including works by George Balanchine, José Limón, Antony Tudor, Bournonville, Pilobolus, and company founder Michael Uthoff. Under artistic director Kirk Peterson, who danced with American Ballet Theater and took over in 1993, the company has

stretched itself even further. Yes, the current rep includes *The Nutcracker* and *Giselle*. But it also features an evening of shorter works by Balanchine, Graham Lustig, and Choo San Goh as well as new pieces by Peterson, Lustig, and Jean Grand-Maitre, all performed at the Bushnell, the company's home base. The School of the Hartford Ballet, begun in 1961, regularly feeds new dancers into the company.

MOMIX

In January 1995, in the midst of the baseball strike, Momix, the witty troupe known for its ability to create surrealistic images with props, light, shadow, and the human body, treated sport-starved New Yorkers to *Baseball*, an evening-length work that tweaked the one-time national pastime. Performed at the New York's Joyce Theater, the work was a huge crossover success, attracting audiences who never attend dance. With its humorous, acrobatic dances, Momix has built an enthusiastic following over its ten-plus-year history. Not surprisingly, troupe founder Moses Pendleton also began Pilobolus, which displays a somewhat similar aesthetic. The name, by the way, from "mixture of Moses," is the trade name for a milk supplement that farm-bred Pendleton once fed his veal calves.

NEW HAVEN BALLET

70 Audubon St., New Haven; (203) 782-9038

New Haven Ballet, with dancers from New Haven Ballet school, stages a full-length classic each year, like *Coppelia* or *The Nutcracker*, choreographed by artistic director Noble Barker and accompanied by musicians from the Wallingford Symphony. The company also recruits guest performers like New York City Ballet dancers Katrina Killian and Philip Neal. Look for seasonal performances at New Haven's Educational Center for the Arts and the Paul Mellon Center for the Performing Arts at Choate-Rosemary Hall in Wallingford.

PILOBOLUS DANCE THEATER

Though based in tiny Washington, Connecticut, Pilobolus spends much of the year on the road, including an annual stint at the American Dance Festival and a summer month at New York's Joyce Theater. This original, if much copied, troupe is well known for witty, athletic, often cerebral dances with a strong sculptural presence. The 1971 creation of Moses Pendelton and Jonathan Wolken, two Dartmouth undergraduates who met in a dance class, it currently has four artistic directors, six dancers, and a large, varied repertory. Recent works include *Collideoscope* set to Corelli's Concert Barocco No. 3, and *Rejoyce*, a lyrical journey through the world of *Finnegans Wake*. The tongue-twister name, by the way, salutes a genus of phototropic fungus.

POLITE SOCIETY

P.O. Box 832, Bloomfield 06002; (860) 286-9191

The performing troupe of the Vintage Dance Society (see Chapter Six), Polite Society's 11-member dance team performs social dances from the Civil War era to speakeasy times in period costumes. The troupe usually dusts off its waltzes, mazurkas, and turkey trots for programs sponsored by the society or at the invitation of other groups. Members also perform at the society's fortnightly dances held at Book-Friends Cafe in Manhattan.

STAMFORD CITY BALLET

50 Atlantic St., Stamford; (203) 964-0506

Formed in 1976 as the American Ballet Academy, Stamford City Ballet stages an annual *Nutcracker* in December, featuring dancers from the school and guest dancers from New York City Ballet, American Ballet Theater, and other professional companies. Their roster of past guests is impressive—Merrill Ashley, Judith Fugate, Susan Jaffe, Darci Kistler, Nikolas Hubbe, Jock Soto, and Damian Woetzel, among others. *The Nutcracker* choreography is pure Balanchine (Stamford City Ballet is one of the companies permitted to use it). Performances are at Stamford's Palace Theater.

CHAPTER THREE

Dance It Yourself: Where To Take Lessons

THIS HEFTY CHAPTER offers a mere taste of the dance classes available in the area. And the quantity of lessons is matched only by the quality. No where else are so many classes taught by working dancers and choreographers or former dancers from the best companies in the world.

Interested in ballroom? Chances are you'll wind up with an instructor who's won an international competition or two or who happens to be the hottest club dancer in town. Want to study modern dance? Choose your technique, be it Limón, Graham, Hawkins, or Cunningham, and sign on at a school founded by the wizard who originated it. And if you're adept at ballet, take an advanced class with one of the masters, like Willem Burmann or David Howard, and share the barre with top dancers from your favorite professional companies.

Not surprisingly, New York's studios range from modest one-room schools to megastudios, with a thicket of practice rooms, dozens of teachers, and classes from morning 'till night. Most, like the classic phrase from *A Chorus Line*, are "up a very steep and narrow stairway." And many, in true urban fashion, are old and cramped, and they have chipping white paint. But looks are deceptive. Some of the best teachers in the world ply their trade in these humble digs.

A quick word on etiquette. Classes can be crowded, so try not to hog the next dancer's space. Observe any dress codes the school may have, and try to get to class on time. Mark combinations with your hands or feet as the instructor explains them; most teachers pay extra attention to students who show signs of life. And if you're an amateur in a class with professionals, don't stand in front of the principal ballerina from American Ballet Theater. She won't appreciate it, and you'll probably learn a lot more watching her instead of gazing at yourself in the mirror.

～ BALLET SCHOOLS AND CLASSES ～

AMERICAN BALLET THEATER
890 Broadway; (212) 477-3030
American Ballet Theater began adult ballet and aerobics classes in its downtown studios in fall 1995. After morning classes for professional dancers, the school offers a variety of day and evening dance classes taught by professional teachers as well as current and former company

dancers. ABT's six big, shabby-genteel studios all have windows, mirrors, moveable barres, and pianos and are well maintained. Call for details.

BALLET ACADEMY EAST

1651 Third Ave.; (212) 410-9140

Around 400 adults, from beginners to near professionals, are enrolled at Ballet Academy East, a seven-year-old school with four big, airy white studios (with columns, unfortunately) and a sharp focus on ballet. Many of the instructors were once performers, and some are dance–world factotums, like choreographer Frances Patrelle, who teaches a lively but tough intermediate ballet class. Jazz and tap are also offered. Fees: single class, $10; eight classes, $72.

BALLET SCHOOL NY

30 E. 31st St.; (212) 679-0401

Ballet School NY, which opened in 1978, offers adult ballet classes, including point, for beginners through professionals, in its elegant wood-wainscotted studio. Instructors include Diana Byer, founder of both the school and its official company, New York Theater Ballet; Sallie Wilson, a former principal dancer with American Ballet Theater, and assorted members of the NYTB company. Students are taught the Cecchetti method of dance, passed on by former ballet mistress Margaret Craske, who retired in 1987 at a ripe 94. Fees: single class, $9; ten classes, $75.

BRONX DANCE THEATER

286 E. 204th St.; (718) 652-7622

One of the few schools of its kind in the Bronx, the Bronx Dance Theater holds adult classes in ballet, modern, jazz, and tap. Billeted in a renovated 1927 movie theater, classes take place in two large studios with suspended wood floors and mirrored walls. Classes also occasionally meet in the school's adjoining theater, which seats 250 and, unfortunately, has no mirrors. Faculty members include school founder Barbara Klein, tapper Jeff Edmond, who also teaches at Steps, and ballet instructor Nadine Ilier. Fees: $50 a month for weekly classes.

THE JOFFREY BALLET SCHOOL/AMERICAN BALLET CENTER
434 Avenue of the Americas; (212) 254-8520
The Joffery School, the official school of the Joffrey Ballet since 1952, is alive and well in Greenwich Village, despite the company's recent move to Chicago. Training is serious, careful, and thorough, particularly for professionals. Through its general program, the school also offers adult classes, from beginning through advanced ballet, as well as point, men's classes, pas de deux, and jazz. The 11-member faculty includes an impressive lineup of former dancers with such companies as the Joffrey, Paris Opera Ballet, Pennsylvania Ballet, San Francisco Ballet, and New York City Ballet. Classes meet in the Joffrey's five white upstairs studios, with windows, mirrors, and Baldwin grand pianos. Fees: single class, $10; ten classes, $95.

THE MANHATTAN BALLET SCHOOL
1556 Third Ave.; (212) 369-3369
For more than 30 years, Manhattan Ballet School has offered classes in classical ballet, including a morning adult class. Participants are mostly former dance students who want to polish their technique and stay in shape. Class meets in the school's large fifth-floor studio, outfitted with a piano and mirrors. Fees: single class, $12; ten classes, $100.

LUCY MOSES SCHOOL FOR MUSIC AND DANCE
129 W. 67th St.; (212) 362-8060
A small number of adult dance classes, including beginning ballet,

aerobic dance, low-impact bodyworks, and the Alexander technique are offered at Lucy Moses. Classes are held in two large studios, with plenty of mirrors and no columns. Fee: 14 classes, $155.

NEUBERT BALLET INSTITUTE

881 Seventh Ave.; (212) 246-3166

This serious school, directed by choreographer Christine Neubert, occupies a handsome piece of skylit turf in the Carnegie Hall Studios. Studios are immaculate, and so is the instruction. The school is best known for ballet, with classes ranging from adult elementary to professional, and specialty courses that include point, variations, pirouette, and pas de deux. The school also offers jazz classes with a special course for teenagers.

NEW YORK BALLET INSTITUTE

1552 Broadway; (212) 730-6933 or (718) 545-7259

A large portrait of the great 19th-century choreographer Marius Petipa gazes from a wall of this new school's snug, white Time Square studio, a reminder of owner/artistic director Ilya Gaft's passion for classical ballet. Classes for professionals, adults and pre-professional girls, ages 11 to 15, are serious and include pas de deux and character dance as well as point and multiple levels of ballet. Besides technique, Gaft, who taught at Russia's prestigious Vaganova State Choreographic Institute, gives students a sense of the culture and history of dance. Fees: single class, $9; ten classes, $80.

NEW YORK CONSERVATORY OF DANCE

30 E. 31st St.; (212) 725-2855

In 1977, Vladimir Dokoudovsky and Patricia Heyes Dokoudovsky opened their classical ballet school specializing in the teachings of the great Russian dancer/teacher Olga Preobrajenska. Simplicity and purity are at the root of the couple's classes, which range from beginner to advanced/professional. Born in Russia, Vladimir danced in the 1930s with the Monte Carlo Ballet Russe, in the 1940s in New York with Ballet Theater, and he choreographed for a variety of companies from the 1950s through 1970s. He's also taught more than 3,000 dancers over the years, he says proudly. His wife and co-director danced with the Metropolitan Opera Ballet and Empire State Ballet. The school has one studio, open to teen and adult students. Fees: single class, $9; ten classes, $80.

NEW YORK SCHOOL OF CLASSICAL DANCE
944 Eighth Ave.; (212) 397-4852

Ballerina Eva Evdokimova often shows up for intermediate classes at the New York School of Classical Dance, which offers several levels of adult and professional ballet classes. Classes are held in the school's midtown studio above McDonald's, and has mirrors, a piano, a tape system, and no columns. In addition to evening adult classes, there's also a (yawn) 7:15 a.m. class. Fees: single class, $10; two lessons a week, $80 a month; three lessons a week, $120 a month.

SCHOOL OF DANCE THEATER OF HARLEM
466 W. 152d St.; (212) 690-2800

Most of the 1,300 students enrolled in the School of Dance Theater of Harlem are children, pre-professional, and professional dancers. But this respected school, begun in 1969 in west Harlem, also offers adult evening classes in a variety of disciplines, including ballet, tap, jazz, and ethnic dance. Classes are held in the company's handsome, newly renovated three-story headquarters in a former auto garage. Fees: single class, $9; ten classes, $80.

∿ MODERN AND CONTEMPORARY ∿
DANCE STUDIOS

MARY ANTHONY DANCE STUDIO

736 Broadway; (212) 674-8191

The Mary Anthony Studio, which opened in 1954, offers a range of modern technique classes, from fundamental and beginner to advanced levels, with an emphasis on training dancers as artists and performers. Technique classes involve floor, center, and barre work to develop strength, flexibility, turnout, placement, and breathing. Most classes feature live piano accompaniments. Besides Anthony, the faculty includes choreographer Anna Sokolow and Bertram Ross, former principal dancer with the Martha Graham Company.

MERCE CUNNINGHAM DANCE STUDIO

55 Bethune St.; (212) 691-9751

Merce Cunningham began choreographing in 1942 and shortly after started teaching his distinct technique, based on strength, clarity, and precision. To properly use the body in performance, Cunningham says dancers must organize and understand its movement. "An enlarging resilience in the mind," as a brochure puts it, is another technique requirement. Besides Cunningham, a spry septuagenarian, instructors include assistant artistic director Chris Komar as well as prominent current and former members of the company. To supplement daily technique classes, from elementary to professional, the studio offers workshops in composition, repertory, rhythm, choreography for the camera, and teaching methods. The pristine white studio with arched windows in the Westbeth artists's complex is the perfect complement to Cunningham's crisp teaching style. Fees: single class, $10; ten classes, $85.

ISADORA DUNCAN FOUNDATION
FOR CONTEMPORARY DANCE

141 W. 26th St.; (212) 691-5040

Classes in all levels of Isadora Duncan technique take place in the Duncan Foundation's large Chelsea studio, which opens onto a terrace (and unfortunately, has columns). A variety of instructors, including foundation founder Lori Belilove, teach to taped classical and New Age music. Fees: single class, $10; ten classes, $80.

MARTHA GRAHAM SCHOOL OF CONTEMPORARY DANCE

316 E. 63d St.; (212) 832-9166

Begun in 1927, the school offers Graham technique classes from beginner to professional for "serious students," as the handsome brochure puts it. No previous training is required for Level 1 classes; admission to higher levels is up to the faculty, which includes members of the Graham company as well as distinguished modern dancers like Maher Benham, Jacqulyn Buglisi, and Yung Yung Tsuai. For aspiring professionals, there's a two-year trainee program. The school also provides intensive summer and winter holiday courses, repertory workshops and classes in composition, music for dancers, and movement for actors (alumni include Kathleen Turner, Gregory Peck, Diane Keaton, and Woody Allen). The school is handsome and, with more than 40 years in the same location, is a tangible chunk of dance history. There are three studios, one large, two small, with white walls, mirrors and, happily, no columns. Fees: single trial class, $10; ten classes, $75; observer's fee, $3.

ERICK HAWKINS SCHOOL OF DANCE

375 West Broadway; (212) 226-5363

The Hawkins school offers four levels of instruction in the so-called free flow modern dance technique Erick Hawkins developed in his 60 or so years as a choreographer and dancer. Taught by company members and associate teachers, classes include fundamentals, advanced beginning, intermediate, and advanced. The school, set in an airy fifth floor SoHo studio, also offers summer and winter intensive workshops, composition, music, and a lecture series. Fees: single class, $10; ten classes, $80.

LIMÓN INSTITUTE
611 Broadway; (212) 777-3353
The Limón Institute is home to Doris Humphrey's famous fall and recovery technique and José Limón's weight-based technique, in which the dancer's weight helps him or her lose and regain balance. Students often get a combination of the two techniques, taught by current and former members of the Limón Company. Classes take place in the company's new columnless, cream-colored studio, which has high ceilings, four walls of high windows, and large mirrors that can demurely disappear behind big creamy curtains. Classes range from beginning through advanced, with intensive courses and workshops, including an annual summer workshop extravaganza at SUNY in Purchase, New York. Fees: single class, $9; ten classes, $80.

MOVEMENT RESEARCH
28 Avenue A; (212) 477-6635
Movement Research holds a full roster of classes in various areas of movement, performance techniques, improvisation, and dance taught by top performers and choreographers like Mia Lawrence, Catherine Sands, David Dorfman, and Sondra Loring. Workshops headed by Eiko & Koma, movement specialist Susan Klein, and Stephanie Skura, among others, are also offered frequently.

NIKOLAIS AND LOUIS DANCE LAB
375 West Broadway; (212) 226-7700

For years the official school of the Nikolais and Murray Louis Dance Company, the Lab, has offered classes in technique, dance theory, improvisation, dance lighting, and a variety of intensive workshops, including a two-week January course and summer courses. But at this writing, the Lab was restructuring, so it's best to call for hours, current courses, and other pertinent details. The faculty includes artistic director Murray Louis as well as current and former dancers with the company.

SOUNDANCE STUDIO
385 Broadway; (212) 941-6457

Opened in 1988, Soundance offers classes in contemporary dance and basic ballet. Dancer Heidi Latski, formerly with the Bill T. Jones/Arnie Zane Company, uses a yoga-based placement technique for her floor exercises, while Sandra Stratton-Gonzalez teaches a more traditional class, based on the Limón technique. The studio has a sprung wood floor, white walls, mirrors, and windows.

PAUL TAYLOR SCHOOL
552 Broadway; (212) 431-5562

Look for sophisticated classes in Paul Taylor technique and repertory in his school's large, mirrorless white studio in a landmark SoHo building. Beginning classes are not offered, so students should have considerable experience in modern dance or ballet before signing on. The faculty ranges from current company members and alumni to artists associated with Taylor, like Canadian solo artist Margie Gillis, sister of the late Taylor dancer/choreographer Christopher Gillis. Other instructors include dancer/choreographer Laura Dean, former Taylor and Ailey dancer Linda Kent, and the venerable Ethel Butler, who taught Taylor during his early days with the Martha Graham Company. Fees: single class, $10; ten classes, $80.

Jazz, Hip-Hop, and Tap Classes
∼ JAZZ ∼

LUIGI'S JAZZ CENTER
300 W. 56th St. (212) 262-4434

Luigi's Jazz Center is just a few blocks from Broadway's biggest musical theaters, which is appropriate. Generations of Broadway dancers, from Donna McKechnie to Liza Minelli, studied with the man many consider to be New York's premiere jazz dance instructor, Luigino Facciuto, a.k.a. Luigi. His story is the stuff of the Hollywood musicals he danced in. At 21, a car accident left him partially paralyzed. To dance again, he developed a stylish movement system that doesn't require full turn-out and rhythmically isolates body parts. He refined his technique working on movie sets with such maestro jazz choreographers as Michael Kidd. Now an agile septuagenerian, Luigi still teaches six days a week. While it's best to know his technique before tackling his intermediate class, his morning style class is for all levels. Luigi's second-floor studio, clean and compact, has mirrors galore, a pale wood floor, hanging plants and and is very urban—like jazz dance. Fees: single class $10, ten classes, $85.

Keep in mind—the megastudios, notably Broadway Dance, Dance Space Inc., New Dance Group Arts Center, and Steps on Broadway—hire superb jazz instructors in a variety of jazz dance strains.

～ HIP-HOP ～

GHETTORIGINAL

(212) 505-0886

Members of this pioneering hip-hop troupe teach classes and workshops in popping, locking, B-boying, and up-rocking at Perry Dance II between performance stints at places like Lincoln Center and Kennedy Center. Veteran dancers Gabriel (Kwikstep) Dionisio, Steve (Wiggles) Clemente, Richard (Crazy Legs) Colon, and Ken (Swift) Gabbert helped shape hip-hop and offer a peek at its history as well as its moves.

BRIAN GREEN

(718) 225-5088

At 24, hip-hop dancer/choreographer/teacher Brian Green has performed in Europe and Japan, staged videos for Mariah Carey and taught for six years, currently at Time Circle Rehearsal Studio, a.k.a. Fazil's. Trained in ballet, tap and African dance, Green deftly mixes complex technique with equally complex street moves—"the immaculate rhythm and foot patterns of tap" with hip-hop's daredevil antics, as he puts it. "You might do 20 jazz turns in one sport, then corkscrew into a split," he says. Club hip-hop, where cutting edge moves are cultivated, is his specialty. "Once you see someone like M.C. Hammer do something, it's commercial, it's old," he says. Green expects his per- forming company, World Soul Inc., to debut in New York sometime in 1996.

DON PHILPOTT

(212) 222-8514

Hip-hop is a state of mind as well as a dance form, according to dancer/teacher Don Philpott. Besides teaching students rudiments of syncopated rhythm and steps straight off the street and MTV, Philpott, who teaches funk aerobics at Bodystrength, imparts an overall understanding of hip-hop's history, from its roots in breakdancing, jazz, and African dance to its singular dress code.

∼ TAP ∼

BRENDA BUFALINO/AMERICAN TAP DANCE ORCHESTRA
(212) 925-3980

She's a different generation from America's classic master tappers like Charles "Honi" Coles and Stanley Brown, but Brenda Bufalino is a tap trailblazer in her own right. Part of the rhythm tap revival of the 1970s, she founded American Tap Dance Orchestra and has traveled the world as tapper and teacher. She taught at Woodpeckers, her Manhattan tap school, until its sad demise in September 1995. But she still teaches in New York through American Tap Dance Orchestra, mostly intermediate and advanced classes. Members of her troupe teach lower levels.

LEON COLLINS TAP DANCE STUDIO
1636A Beacon St., Brookline, Massachusetts 02146;
(617) 232-0105

Yes, it's in Massachusetts, but rhythm tappers swear by this one-room studio near Boston, begun in 1977 by master tapper Leon Collins. Unlike most top tappers of his generation, Collins was as interested in teaching as performing and devised a instruction system, based on music, that's still used at his school. The school, which attracts beginners and professionals alike, keeps Collins's routines alive. Pros from New York and even from overseas drop in for a few brush-up sessions. The six faculty members include school directors Dianne Walker and Pamela Raff, former members of Collins & Co., Leon Collins's performing troupe.

HEATHER CORNELL

(212) 787-7181

As artistic director of Manhattan Tap, Cornell choreographs and performs the rhythm tap numbers that distinguish her troupe. She also teaches two intensive courses in Manhattan, usually in the summer and winter. Classes include instruction in technique, choreography, and improvisation and usually feature live music.

JANE GOLDBERG

(212) 393-1182 or (500) 675-8661

Jane Goldberg learned her craft directly from New York's swing era master tappers—John Bubbles, Charles "Honi" Coles, Charles "Cookie" Cook. So she teaches traditional tap with complex footwork rooted in rhythm. Besides private lessons, Goldberg also teaches tap and tap history at New York University. She tailors instruction to individual requirements. Goldberg compares the sound of tapping feet to the sound of a jazz instrument; everyone has an individual sound. She also does a comedy act, called "Rhythm and Schmooze," which she has performed at LaMama, among other places. Fees: lessons from $50 to $100.

MARK GOODMAN

(212) 946-1848

A former rhythm tapper with American Tap Dance Orchestra, Goodman went out on his own several years ago and has since danced in concert with Gregory Hines and in his own show at Carnegie Hall. Besides offering private lessons, Goodman teaches at Steps and at Broadway Dance Center. His teaching style blends rhythm tap with show tap "so it's not just the feet that move," he says. His music choices are somewhat unconventional by tap standards—lots of Harry Connick, Jr. and Basia with some Frank Sinatra-style classics tossed in.

CHUCK GREEN
(212) 541-4455

Master tapper Chuck Green qualifies as one of tap's most devoted teachers—ever. During a recent illness, he had his students smuggle him out of the hospital so he could teach his weekly Saturday class at Fazil's. A rhythm tapper supreme, Green teaches group classes. Fee: single class, $15.

LISA HOPKINS
(212) 874-2410

Lisa Hopkins teaches jazz and rhythm tap at Steps, and tries to give both sets of students the elements they often lack. Jazz dancers need to be stretched rhythmically, like tap dancers, she says. And tap students need to learn to dance with the entire body, the way jazz dancers do. A former dancer with Manhattan Tap, Hopkins teaches to rhythmic music from the 1940s through the 1990s.

HERVÉ LE GOFF
(212) 501-2237

Hervé Le Goff learned rhythm tap in his native France and since moving to New York in 1989 has danced with American Tap Dance Orchestra and Tap Express. These days he has a solo act, tapping with a pianist. He also teaches at Steps. Le Goff's classes are always taught to Latin music, which you also hear on his voice mail. "When you hear it, you want to move," he says. Le Goff studied with both Jimmy Slyde protege Sara Petronio and the ubiquitous Brenda Bufalino.

MAX POLLAK
(212) 932-8668

Vienna native Max Pollak decided to become a tap dancer when he saw a Fred Astaire movie at age five. After studying in Austria, he headed for New York, joined Manhattan Tap, and now teaches at the New School's Mannes College. For his music students at Mannes, Pollak teaches tap as percussive music, writing out steps on sheet music. He also dances with pianist Danilo Perez's Latin jazz group "as their percussionist," he says, and offers private lessons. Fee: $40 an hour.

PEGGY SPINA STUDIO
115 Prince St.; (212) 674-8885

Peggy Spina started tap at age four in southern California, and despite 20 years as a performer and teacher of modern dance, she calls tap her first love. Since 1977, she has taught in her SoHo loft with its exquisite maple floor. She studied with tap masters Charles "Honi" Coles, Baby Lawrence, and Chuck Green, and since 1977, has given both group and private lessons. Spina combines traditional tap with steps from her modern dance background. Besides teaching, Spina performs with her five-woman company, the Peggy Spina Tap Company, gives concerts in her 55-seat studio, and holds workshops featuring tap masters like Coles and Green. Fees: single group classes, $13 to $14; private lessons, $50 an hour.

ROBIN TRIBBLE
(212) 691-8972

Robin Tribble, whose company Tap Express performs throughout the city, also teaches rhythm tap at Steps, Broadway Dance Center, and the Connecticut Ballet in Stamford. She likes teaching to music ranging from early jazz to swing, bee-bop, and Latin jazz.

～ BALLROOM DANCE CLASSES ～
AND SCHOOLS

AEQUUS DANCE STUDIO

207 East 84th Street; (212) 650-0881

One of New York's oldest ballroom studios, Aeguus was started in 1977 by Carlan Russell and Carla Sheinkopf, who teach all types of social ballroom dance, from foxtrot to Texas two-step. Most lessons are private, with one group class each week. Russell's specialty is teaching people who take up dancing as physical therapy following a stroke, heart attack, or other illness. Fees: single classes, $9; private lessons, $60 an hour.

FRED ASTAIRE DANCE STUDIOS

666 Broadway; (212) 475-7776
303 E. 43rd St.; (212) 697-6535
157 E. 86th St.; (212) 348-4430
2182 Broadway; (212) 595-3200
1300 Hylan Boulevard, Staten Island; (718) 668-1300
1301 W. 7th St., Brooklyn; (718) 382-3479
118-12 Queens Blvd., Forest Hills, Queens; (718) 544-0911
207-20 Northern Blvd., Bayside, Queens; (718) 225-1980

The Fred Astaire Dance Studios celebrated their fiftieth anniversary in 1995, and New York's franchises are in good shape. Private lessons in all styles of ballroom and Latin dance are the house specialty. Though most students are interested primarily in social dancing, the studios teach a standardized curriculum that preps dancers for international- and American-style competitions. Most teachers are competition veterans. At Astaire's West Side studio, for example, directors Darius and Jolanta Mosteika and Theo Derleth are all champs. Besides passing a certification test, Astaire instructors take daily brush-up sessions on the latest steps. Each franchise is a bit different, though Derleth says his West Side outpost, with its large, spotless studio is typical.

BALLROOM DANCENTRE
939 Eighth Ave.; (212) 581-2640
Held in a large, white, second-floor studio, Richard & Bonnie Diaz's Ballroom Dancentre offers weekly classes in almost everything—social dancing, Latin nightclub dance, competition-style ballroom and Latin American, Argentine tango, country western, swing, and more. The directors Diaz, America's first world mambo champions in 1989, head a superb faculty that includes tango dancers Danel & Maria and mambo king Eddie Torres. Students are invited to free practice sessions and monthly socials. Fees: single classes, $12.50; private lessons, $45 to $60.

MARGARET BATIUCHOK
238 E. 14th St.; (212) 598-0154 or (718) 358-2050
With a background in modern dance, jazz, ballet, tap and ballroom, Margaret Batiuchok can teach almost any kind of ballroom, from country western to Argentine tango. But her specialty is swing and its numerous strains, from Lindy hop to West Coast. "It's an American dance form, and the music really drives you," she says, explaining swing's current appeal. Batiuchok, a founding member of the New York Swing Dance Society, wrote her master's thesis on Lindy at New York University and has taught for ten years, both group and private lessons. She also gives workshops on partnering and the necessary skills for dancing. Fees: group classes, $15; private lessons, $60 an hour.

SANDRA CAMERON DANCE CENTER
20 Cooper Square; (212) 674-0505
Social ballroom dancing is the main focus at the school started in 1979

by Sandra Cameron, a former U.S. professional ballroom champion. The studio, which recently moved to new, larger headquarters, offers instruction in all levels of everything from Viennese waltz to country western. Around 20 students are in each class, and they need not register with a partner—"they're constantly changing partners in class," says Lawrence Schulz, studio director. This is an excellent studio for novices who want to feel at ease dancing at weddings and clubs. Classes in jazz and tap are also offered, as are private lessons and competition coaching. Fees: four-week ballroom course, $60; private lessons, $60 an hour.

KITTY CONCANNON

(212) 924-9630

Long-time ballroom instructor Kitty Concannon teaches all types of social dance, but she specializes in pre-marriage coaching for nervous couples who want to feel comfortable dancing at their wedding. Often this means choreographing a special dance to the couple's favorite song. Sometimes she coaches the entire wedding party.

DANCE MANHATTAN

39 W. 19th St.; (212) 807-0802

Though just three years old, this big, ambitious school specializes in social dance instruction. With 17 seasoned teachers, it's not unusual to see ten classes a night in everything from the blue plate special (waltz, foxtrot, tango, rumba) to tap for kicks. Classes can be highly specific—Roseland foxtrot, Palladium mambo, gay and lesbian survival swing. Big specialties include Argentine tango, with guest teachers from Argentina, and all types of swing, hot-hot at the moment. Owners Elena Iannucci and Teddy Kern, a longtime dancer/choreographer, recruit prominent guest instructors in West Coast swing from all over the country. The school recently moved to a huge new downtown studio (10,000 square feet), where it also holds social dance parties —tango on Monday nights; ballroom, swing, Latin, and hustle on Friday nights. Parties are open to the public. Fee: four-week course, $60.

DANCE NEW YORK
237 W. 54th St.; (212) 246-5797

With its two peach-colored studios and drapey maroon curtains, Dance New York offers a lightly glamourous backdrop for the ballroom instructors who rent space for classes. Opened in February 1995, this upstairs theater–district studio offers classes in social dance as well as group and private instuction in both international- and American-style competitive dance. Though new, the space has already attracted top teachers, including ballroom dance/choreography factotum Peter DiFalco. The studio also rents space to ballet instructor Carol Rioux and jazz instructor Jeremy Peterson. Fee: $10 to $15 a class.

DANCESPORT
1845 Broadway; (212) 307-1111

This lively upstairs ballroom school with 30 instructors, over 70 group classes a week, and private lessons galore, offers a little something for almost everyone. You can learn social dancing, club dancing, or the international and American styles of competitive dancing. And almost every ballroom style is taught, from salsa/mambo, West Coast swing and rumba to international foxtrot, hustle, and country western. Tango—Argentine, American, and international—is a DanceSport specialty; owner Paul Pellicoro, one of New York's top ballroom teachers, choreographed Al Pacino's famous tango scene in *Scent of a Woman* and teaches tango along with other Latin styles at his ten-year-old studio. This is an excellent place for beginners. The school also holds free nightly practice parties. Fees: four group classes, $65; private lessons, $55 to $70.

DANEL & MARIA
(718) 325-6579

Tango master Danel was raised on tango in his native Argentina. And tango is in his partner Maria's blood as well, he says, even though she's from Italy. The two met 30 years ago in a dance class, married, and currently reign as one of tango's premiere couples. In New York, they teach at Sandra Cameron Dance Center, Ballroom Dancentre, and Dorothy's Dance Center in Mount Vernon; they offer private lessons as well. Danel also dispenses a little tango philosophy. His tango is not the slick, codified dance seen in international competitions but that of the Argentine *milonga*, or dance hall. He encourages students to cultivate their own styles, improvising to tango's earthy, soulful music. Tango's sensuous, stylized movements are from the waist down, with no opposition; the man and woman use the same foot at the same time. The man plots the course, and in Danel & Maria's case, the results are divine.

EDDIE DORFER AND MERCEDES COLON
(718) 591-2643

For Eddie and Mercedes, the 1985 visit by Tango Argentino, the thrilling South American tango troupe, was a revelation. "Tango changed our lives," Dorfer says. It certainly changed what he teaches and dances. A longtime teacher of Latin and ballroom dance, he threw himself into tango, studied with members of the Argentine troupe and, with his wife, Mercedes, became one of New York's premiere tango performers. Dorfer's specialty is Argentine tango, with its haunting music and improvisational possibilities, but he also teaches American tango and cafe-style tango, danced on small spaces. Fee: $50 an hour.

PIERRE DULAINE

213 E. 82nd St.; (212) 532-8091

As co-artistic director of American Ballroom Theater, the popular ensemble that performs ballroom dance concerts, Pierre Dulaine trains some of the most accomplished ballroom pros in the land. But Dulaine, a four-time winner of the prestigious British National Championships with partner Yvonne Marceau, also offers private lessons for "ordinary couples," as he puts it. Students learn whatever social ballroom dances they choose—waltz, tango, quick step, merengue, samba, swing and so forth. Dulaine also coaches dancers for competitions.

FIFTH AVENUE BALLROOM

319 Fifth Avenue; (212) 532-6232

Since it opened in 1993, this attractive midtown studio, with its skylit fourth floor ballroom, has offered a large menu of classes in social and competitive dancing, both American and international styles. The 15-member faculty includes dance master Robert DiFalco, as well as a range of experts in Latin and ballroom strains. Beginners can try the basic sampler (foxtrot, waltz, rumba, cha cha) or something a bit sexier like merengue, swing, salsa, or club Latin, which includes tango. There's also a waltz class with Viennese waltz instruction included. Free Friday night socials for students. Fees: four classes, $60; private classes, $52 to $62 an hour.

TITO PUENTE & EDDIE TORRES SCHOOL
FOR THE PERFORMING ARTS

939 Eighth Ave.; (718) 824-3950 (temporary number)

This Latin music and dance school is new, but the co-owners are near legends in their respective fields. Though bandleader Puente is better known, Latin dance enthusiasts know Torres as one of the mambo's most thrilling innovators. These days, mambo is ultra-hot, due in part to what Torres terms its "very sultry, romantic, and passionate moves." The mambo's recent revival has meant a name change—it's now called salsa. "Salsa means sauce," Torres sniffs. But mambo translates into "nice juicy gossip," he explains. "Someone would say, 'I've got a mambo for you.'". Whatever it's called, it's still danced to the sensuously joyous rhythms of Afro-Cuban music. Torres teaches his own technique—300 steps and 150 turn patterns performed in whatever order the dancer chooses. Torres's new school offers a full repertory of group classes in Latin dances including tango, rumba, samba, and paso doble, with an emphasis on social, not competitive dance.

STEPPING OUT
1780 Broadway; (212) 245-5200
This large, upstairs studio underwent intensive renovations during summer 1995, but that didn't seem to dissuade the students who turn up for social and competitive (international and American styles) dance lessons. The school offers all the basics, from introduction to the international style to beginning salsa and merengue. But as a large studio, Stepping Out also holds specialty classes, including Palladium mambo, a style popularized in the 1950s, and a full program for gays and lesbians. There's also a technique class on arm styling. The school, opened in 1985, brings in guest instructors and stages workshops. Fees: four classes, $60; private lessons, $57 to $67 an hour.

STRICTLY BALLROOM
139 E. 57th St.; (212) 832-5872
This midtown school, with its elegant studio, specializes in private lessons. Students can choose from a course of private lessons in any ballroom or Latin discipline or can blend private and group lessons.

Classes range from basic social dance-style ballroom (foxtrot and rumba or waltz and mambo) to international style classes in competitive dance. There are also Latin club classes (merengue and salsa). Fees: four private lessons with free practice session, $252 to $280; four private and four group classes, $288 to $320.

THE YWCA AT 53RD & LEXINGTON
610 Lexington Ave.; (212) 735-9753
The East Side megastudio offers a full range of social dance instruction including country and western, Latin, and classic ballroom. Social dances are held Tuesdays, Thursdays, and Fridays.

~ ETHNIC DANCE SCHOOLS ~
AND CLASSES

AMERICAN SPANISH DANCE THEATER/ANDREA DEL CONTE
144 E. 24th St.; (212) 674-6725
Flamenco performer Andrea Del Conte, artistic director of American Spanish Dance Theater, teaches a range of flamenco classes, beginning through advanced. Del Conte, who visits Spain every year to hone her craft, offers group and private lessons at Lotus Music & Dance Studios and New York Open Center.

BALLET HISPANICO SCHOOL OF DANCE
167 W. 89th St.; (212) 362-6710
The Ballet Hispanico School of Dance offers classes in both ballet and flamenco to young students, but adults can take only flamenco. Classes are held in the company's handsome West Side headquarters in a pair of renovated carriage houses. The four studios are well lit and spacious with cushioned wood floors. Fees: single class, $9; five classes, $40.

PAT CANNON
(914) 753-6950

Though based upstate, Pat Cannon rents space in New York to offer private instruction in numerous all-American dance styles, including clogging, country dancing, square dancing, Texas two-step, and cajun dancing. Cannon, whose Foot and Fiddle Dance Company performs professionally, also gives private instruction to groups.

DJONIBA DANCE & DRUM CENTER
37 E. 18th St.; (212) 477-3464

This downtown studio, founded and directed by Djoniba Mouflet, specializes in a dazzling range of ethnic dance classes, including African, Haitian, Cuban, Samba-Jazz, Brazilian, and capoeira, the Brazilian martial art that combines dance and music. Additional classes are held in ballet, hip-hop, flamenco, and Dunham-technique modern dance. The school also stages monthly performances by visiting dancers and musicians. Recent offerings included troupes from Guinea and the Ivory Coast. Fees: single class, $9 to $11; ten–class card, $80 to $100.

FARETA SCHOOL OF DANCE & DRUM
622 Broadway; (212) 677-6708

Vivid African-style murals bedeck the narrow hallway leading to Fareta's windowless basement studio. And though long and narrow, the wood-floor studio provides ample space for some of the city's best classes in ethnic dance. Offerings include African, Afro-Caribbean, Afro-Haitian, Haitian, and Brazilian dance as well as capoeira. There are also two modern classes—Dunham technique and modern technique with dancer/choreographer Ron Brown. Fees: single class, $9; discounts available for multiple classes.

LOTUS MUSIC & DANCE

109 W. 27th St.; (212) 627-1076

Originally a school of dance from India, Lotus currently qualifies as the United Nations of studios, with an impressive roster of international dance classes, each taught by a top performer from a different country. U Win Maung, a second-generation Burmese traditional dancer, has performed for 25 years. And Potri Ranka Manis, a published poet *and* a princess, teaches Philippine tribal dances. The school also includes instruction in flamenco, South Indian dance, or Bharata Natyam, North Indian dance, or Odissi, Hawaiian dance, and Korean dance. In addition, the studio hosts frequent dance peformances and workshops by traditional artists, from flamenco to butoh. The school, with four studios, also offers classes in less exotic disciplines, such as jazz, tap, ballroom dance, and salsa aerobics. Fees: single class, $10; discounts for mulitple classes.

LILIANA MORALES

(212) 472-7394

A popular flamenco performer, both with Flamenco Latino and as a solo dancer, Liliana Morales studied flamenco in Spain and has taught for years. Though she often garnishes her flamenco with Hispanic and other influences in performance, she teaches the pure stuff, emphasizing technique. Look for Morales's classes at Time Circle Rehearsal Studio, a.k.a. Fazil's, and MTW Studios at 440 Lafayette Street. Fee: $13.

SERENA STUDIOS

939 Eighth Ave.; (212) 247-1051; (212) 245-9603

Serena teaches Middle Eastern dancing at her upstairs midtown studio. Her technique blends the basics of oriental dance, as derived from its Arabic and Turkish origins, with the rhythmic patterns of Middle

Eastern music. Grace and coordination are emphasized, she says. Serena's background is Hungarian Gypsy, but she studied dance with Ruth St.Denis *and* in the Middle East, has performed with Middle Eastern musicians, and currently oversees the Egyptian Folkloric show at Manhattan's Cleopatra Club. Fees: single class, $8, ten classes, $70.

And keep in mind—the megastudios, notably Time Circle Rehearsal Studio and Alvin Ailey American Dance Center, offer a wide variety of ethnic dance classes.

∼ SKATE DANCING SCHOOLS AND CLASSES ∼

LEZLY SKATE SCHOOL
(212) 777-3232
Lezly Ziering dances on and off skates, but quad and in-line skaters know him as one of skate-dancing's master teachers. Classes are set to music and structured much like wheel–less dance classes, "half technique, half movement," Lezly says. Both quad and in-line skaters are welcome, though most people find it easier to dance, and balance, on quads. Three-wheel blades, which can be custom made, are preferred for dancing. Classes range from New York disco to freestyle jazz dance. Lezly teaches at Roxy Rink and T'ai Chi Dance and Skate Rehearsal Studios.

ROLLER RINKS AT CHELSEA PIERS
23rd St. at Hudson River; (212) 336-6200
The new Roller Rinks offers two dance classes on skates. Rollaerobics, taught by Margarett Dykstra of the dance troupe NYC Skating Crew, is an aerobic workout that teaches in-liners rhythm and move construction. Hip-Hop Dance, taught by NYC Skating Crew founder Diane

Goldberg, features the latest hip-hop steps with complex step formations like those tossed off by the in-line dancers at Central Park flats. Fees: single class, $15 with skate rental; ten classes, $112 without skate rental.

SCHOOL OF THE ICE THEATER OF NEW YORK

23rd St. at Hudson River; (212) 336-6100

Ice Theater of New York holds several levels of classes for ice skaters eager to learn theatrical moves and routines at its new home at Chelsea Piers. Group classes, like ballet classes, offer technique and develop musicality. Teachers include Moira North, a founding member of Ice Theater of New York, and Rob McBrien, a United States figure skating gold medalist who directed the John Curry Company. For absolute beginners, North suggests the Learn-to-Skate classes offered by Sky Rink. The New School for Social Research also hold an introductory class in ice dancing. Fees: eight-week session, $125.

∼ THERAPEUTIC DANCE ∼

GELABERT STUDIOS

257 W. 86th St.; (212) 874-7188

Raoul Gelabert has taught ballet for over 40 years. But many of his clients visit his Upper West Side studio for his expertise in injury prevention through correct technique. A physical therapist with a Ph.D. in biomechanics, and author of *Raoul Gelabert's Anatomy for the Dancer*, Gelabert works individually with clients to discover an injury's cause, be it tendonitis, foot problems, whatever. "It's usually related to the way the dancer works," he says. Some stay on and take his relaxing ballet and exercise classes.

SUSAN KLEIN SCHOOL OF DANCE
48 Beach St.; (212) 226-6510

"It's a rough sport," says Susan Klein, who learned the hard way. At 19, an injury ended her promising dance career and she decided to explore the workings of the body, how it heals and how injury can be prevented. The result became the Klein Technique. Classes teach dancers to move correctly, both to prevent injury or to promote healing once an injury occurs. Klein's classes, built around stretching and standing floor work, have a loyal following, particularly among members of downtown post-modern companies like those of Trisha Brown and Bebe Miller. Fees: single class, $10; ten classes, $80.

THE PILATES STUDIO
2121 Broadway; (212) 875-0189

Since its creation in the 1920s by Joseph Pilates, dancers have championed this gravity-defying exercise method using mats and spring-loaded machines. And Sean Gallagher's Pilates studio, in the same building as megastudio Steps on Broadway, is a dancer's favorite. With 15 certified Pilates instructors, clients can receive one-on-one instruction on the machines or sign on for group classes on mats. Fee: mat classes, $15.

ZENA ROMMETT FLOOR-BARRE TECHNIQUE
(212) 874-2410; (212) 777-8067

Some 30 years ago, Zena Rommett devised her trademarked floor-barre method, designed to correct alignment, control the pelvis, build strength and flexibility, and facilitate ballet technique. But dancers in all fields, from ballet and modern to jazz hoofers and ice skaters, take classes with Rommet and her disciples at Dance Space and Steps. A high percentage of students are professional dancers recovering from injuries, but often students come just to get stronger and indulge in an exercise program that feels good.

∼ MEGASTUDIOS ∼

ALVIN AILEY AMERICAN DANCE CENTER
211 W. 61st St.; (212) 767-0940

Just 125 students signed up at the Alvin Ailey American Dance Center when it opened in Brooklyn in 1969, but these days this impressive school, with its brick interior walls and windows overlooking treetops, is one of Manhattan's biggest and best. Over 3,000 students, from children and professionals to adults who just want exercise, are enrolled in more than 150 weekly classes. This is one-stop shopping for dance. It's also in keeping with the Ailey company philosophy that dancers should possess a variety of technical skills. The ballet department boasts a seven-member faculty including former members of American Ballet Theater, New York City Ballet, Dance Theater of Harlem and, of course, the Ailey troupe. The nine-member modern dance faculty includes specialists in Graham-, Horton-, and Dunham-based techniques. Students can also study jazz and tap dance, Spanish, East Indian, and African dance, body conditioning and yoga. Classes in dance academics—dance history, music, and theater arts—are offered as well. Live music, from piano to African drums, accompany classes. With a slew of studios, including two big ones named for Ailey and artistic director Judith Jamison, a Capezio boutique, and seminars on nutrition and injury prevention, the place positively bustles. Fees: single class, $9; ten classes, $80.

BROADWAY DANCE CENTER
1733 Broadway; (212) 582-9304

Big, brisk, cramped, and impersonal, Broadway Dance is a classic New York megastudio. To reach the narrow spiral staircase connecting its two floors, you elbow past crowds at the front desk and step over dancers clustered on the floor outside the studios, awaiting the next class. But these big-city annoyances hardly dissuade the masses who show up for the studio's 50-odd classes each day. Twin lures are the near encyclopedic range of classes taught by some of the best instructors in town, including a hefty percentge of working dancers and choreographers. The resulting participants range from dancers in Broadway shows and professional ballerinas to eager amateurs who like soaking up the energy-charged atmosphere. Key concentrations are ballet, jazz and tap, and though the atmosphere seems more Broadway than Lincoln Center, two of New York's most respected ballet instructors teach here, Madame Darvash and Finis Jhung. Tap classes range from Broadway to rhythmn (the superb Savion Glover and Barbara Duffy teach the latter). Jazz classes are equally diverse, from Frank Hatchett's intermediate/advanced to hip-hop with Rebel of the Home Boys. Additional classes include modern, ballroom, flamenco, Afro-Brazil aerobics, Spanish, African, and Reggae-cise. Broadway Dance also encompasses Ballet Arts at City Center, 130 West 56th Street; (212) 582-3350 (class cards can be used at both locations). This smaller outpost, in business since 1937, offers multiple levels of ballet, tap, jazz, Spanish dance, and Afro-Brazillian aerobics. Fees: single class, $11; ten classes, $100.

DANCE SPACE INC.

622 Broadway; (212) 777-8067

After a ride to the sixth floor in a claustrophobia-inducing elevator, Dance Space turns into one of the more pleasant megastudios in town — five oddly angled white rooms with hardwood floors, brick walls and mirrors galore. It started small in 1984 with two studios where Lynn Simonson, a founder, taught her Simonson jazz technique, designed to prevent injury through proper alignment and an awareness of how the body moves. Simonson, co-founder Laurie DeVito, and six other faculty members still teach Simonson jazz, but the studio has swelled to include classes in ballet, modern dance (Horton, Lewitsky and Limón techniques), African dance, yoga, Alexander technique, Pilates-based workouts, even hula. But the studio is perhaps best known for its monthly modern guest artists, an impressive bunch that has included Ron Brown, David Dorfman, Stephen Petronio, Doug Elkins, Dwight Rhoden and Kevin Wynn. Each month four different guests each teach for a week. Fees: single class, $9.50; ten classes, $85.

GOWANUS ARTS EXCHANGE

295 Douglass St., Brooklyn; (718) 596-5250

Gowanus offers a variety of classes in theater, writing, and dance, including modern dance, jazz, ballet, African, and creative movement.

CHARLES MOORE DANCE STUDIO

397 Bridge St., Brooklyn; (718) 467-7127

This Brooklyn megastudio offers topflight classes in ballet, modern jazz, and tap with a special emphasis on African dance, including Afro-Caribbean and Ivory Coast/Senegalese dance. The center occupies two big studios and is affiliated with the Charles Moore Dance Theater, a fine performing company specializing in African ethnic dance.

NEW DANCE GROUP ARTS CENTER

254 W. 47th St.; (212) 719-2733

It took this theater district megastudio a long time to rebuild after a fire decimated its five-story building in 1991. And the process is not quite complete; the children's program and pedagogical division haven't yet returned, though artistic director Rick Schussell expects to have the kid's division running by summer 1996. In the meantime, New Dance Group's studios bustle with open classes that attract over 1,000 students—multiple levels of ballet, point, body conditioning, yoga, martial arts, and a vast number of classes in jazz and tap, all taught by working dancers and choreographers. (This is a Broadway dance studio, after all.) Both theater tap and rhythm tap are offered, the latter taught by Sherry Eyster, a member of American Tap Dance Orchestra. In addition, Broadway shows often use the center's studios for rehearsals (you can drop by almost any day and witness a real life version of *A Chorus Line*). Begun in 1932, the center has a fascinating history. Charles Weidman and Doris Humphrey, among others, danced here, instructors like Bessie Schönberg taught choreography, and students included Jerome Robbins and Eliot Feld. Fees: single class, $9; ten classes, $80.

92nd STREET Y
Lexington Ave. at 92nd St.; (212) 996-1100
The ultimate Upper East Side megastudio, the Y became a serious dance center when it merged with the Harkness Foundation after Harkness House closed in 1985. But well before that, its studios served as rehearsal, teaching, and performance spaces for some of dance's most distinguished names, including Doris Humphrey, Agnes De Mille, Anna Sokolow, Robert Joffrey, and Alvin Ailey. Besides its two studios, the center features a library, lounge, fitness center, babysitting services and classes, classes, classes. Basics, available in all levels, include ballet, modern, Isadora Duncan technique, jazz dance, tap, ballroom, Alexander technique, Afro-Caribbean, spinal gymnastics, and dance exercise as well as special mature adult classes for people with Parkinson's disease and other movement disorders. The first-rate faculty has included tapper Jeff Edmond and the superb Hawkins dancer Catherine Tharin, with professional workshops taught by Eiko & Koma, Urban Bush Women, and David Gordon. The Y also offers lecture series with top dancers and choreographers.

PERRY DANCE II

132 Fourth Ave.; (212) 505-0886

When choreographer Igal Perry moved his 11-year-old Peridance Center to new, larger digs in 1994, he changed its name (to Perry Dance II), increased the number of studios (four large, one small), and adopted the earmarks of a megastudio (big faculty, lots of classes, frequent workshops, guest instructors). Numerous classes in ballet and modern dance form its core, but the center also offers jazz, hip-hop, strength/alignment, and tae kwon do. Ballet classes attract both serious dancers (Perry teaches a morning professional class) and adults who just want to stay in shape. The nine-member ballet faculty includes Charles Anderson, artistic director of Ballet Inc., and Jan Miller, whose classes stress strength and stamina. And each summer, members of the Royal Danish Ballet teach a workshop in Bournonville technique. Besides five permanent modern dance instructors, recent guest teachers have included choreographer Kevin Wynn and Megan Williams of the Mark Morris Dance Group. Perry Dance II is also home to the Jennifer Muller Company, whose members teach Muller's technique, emphasizing breath, energy, fluidity, and control. Fees: single class, $10; ten classes, $85.

SPOKE THE HUB DANCING

748 Union St., Brooklyn; (718) 857-5158

This lively arts organization offers classes at Prospect Park Picnic House and 295 Douglass Street as well as its impressive new Re-Creation Center at the above address. Faculty includes a number of performing dancers, like Spoke the Hub founder Elise Long and rhythm tapper Sherry Eyster of American Tap Dance Orchestra. Among the classes are modern technique and improv, Afro-Caribbean, ballroom, Isadora Duncan dance, jazz, tap, postnatal exercise, and theater workshops. Fee: one class a week for 12 weeks, $120.

STEPS ON BROADWAY
2121 Broadway; (212) 874-2410

Studios don't get much more mega than this. Though detractors call it the factory, aficionados—and there are plenty—love the place for its brisk atmosphere, six crowded studios, and enormous faculty comprising almost exclusively working dancers and choreographers. The numbers are awesome—40 to 50 classes a day, seven days a week, taught by 88 instructors—and that doesn't include top-flight guest teachers like Fernando Bujones, Maya Plisetskaya, Ann Reinking, Dwight Rhoden, Desmond Richardson, Margo Sappington, and Lynn Seymour. Students can be pretty awesome, too. Professional ballet dancers, including a healthy representation from American Ballet Theater, flock to classes taught by Willelm Burmann and Michael Vernon, among others, and the jazz classes, taught by standouts like Joe Lanteri, Michael Owens, and Suzi Taylor, are popular with pros, from dancers in Broadway shows to the Rockettes. Steps, still run by founders Carol Paumgarten and Patrice Soriero, started small in 1979 with just four classes. Today its offerings encompass multilevel classes in ballet, jazz, modern/modern jazz, tap (rhythm and Broadway), theater dance, modern Brazillian, flamenco, hip-hop, yoga, and fitness. All this and a compact Capezio boutique, too. Fees: single class, $10; ten classes, $90.

TIMES CIRCLE REHEARSAL STUDIOS (formerly Fazil's)
743 Eighth Ave.; (212) 541-4455

The bannisters are rickety, the paint is peeling, and the lighting is eerie, but this theater district nest of 13 studios attracts some of New York's top teachers, particularly in Spanish and Middle Eastern dance and tap. It's also downright historical. Jimmy Cagney practiced here, and in the film *Easter Parade*, Fred Astaire talked about rehearsing at Michael's, as the studio was then called. Though the place officially became Time Circle Rehearsal Studios several years ago, dancers still call it Fazil's (that's also the name on the front door), after its mustachioed owner. Instructors rent space, so there's no monthly catalog of classes. Instead, students drop by to check out the teachers' bulletin board or call. Longtime teachers include tap master Chuck Green, Middle Eastern dance instructors Elena, Yousry Sharif, and Sa'adia and Asemara, hip-hop master Brian Green, Spanish dancers José Molina, Recompa, Victorio La Meira, and La Conja as well as assorted visiting instructors from Spain.

WEST SIDE DANCE PROJECT
162 W. 83rd St.; (212) 580-0915
This studio offers a wide range of classes in ballet, jazz, tap, modern dance, and exercise, including Basic Bodyworks, a synthesis of dance, yoga, and exercise techniques. Fee: eight classes, $64.

THE YWCA AT 53RD & LEXINGTON
610 Lexington Ave.; (212) 735-9753
Besides its vast array of ballroom offerings, the YW dance center holds a wide range of classes and workshops in ballet, tap, flamenco, jazz, hip-hop, Afro-Caribbean, modern, and Middle Eastern dance. Fee: ten hour-long classes, $89.

~ **CHAPTER FOUR** ~

Dance Kids New York

ONE OF THE NEAT THINGS about being a kid in New York is the unparalleled selection of dance classes. The options start early; two-year-olds, too young to indulge in pee wee softball or piano lessons, can take creative movement classes with mom or sit out a year and sign on for pre-ballet at three.

Older children have boundless options—ballet, modern, jazz, African, clogging, even specialized techniques, like Isadora Duncan or Martha Graham. And for serious wanna-bes, institutions like the School of American Ballet, the Joffrey School, and the Alvin Ailey

American Dance Center are as good as it gets, attracting students from all over the world. (It's just a lot more convenient if you commute to class from the West Side.)

Given this choice, making the proper selection can be challenging. Most kids want lessons because dancing is fun, as well as a painless way to develop discipline, etiquette, musicality, and strength. For those with a career in the offing, choosing the right school is vital; poor technique learned young is hard to remedy. But this being New York, there is no shortage of excellent schools—and no shortage of concerned onlookers offering advice.

∼ DANCE CLASSES ∼

ALVIN AILEY AMERICAN DANCE CENTER
211 W. 61st St.; (212) 767-0940
The Junior Division, for students ages three to 15, is a key component of the Ailey Center. The littlest ones start with "First Steps," a course of creative dance, mime, music, and drama and at seven, proceed to the pre-professional program of ballet and West African dance. Graded classes in ballet, tap, modern, point, Spanish dance, mime (for girls), and gymastics (for boys) follow. Options abound for students ages 15 to 23 interested in professional careers. The school has sent students into a variety of professional companies, including New York City Ballet, Frankfurt Ballet, and, of course, the Ailey company.

BALLET ACADEMY EAST
1651 Third Ave.; (212) 410-9140
Though Ballet Academy East opened in 1988, it qualifies as something of a New York institution. The school grew out of the Fokine School, operated for years by Christine Fokine, a former daughter-in-law of

famed Russian choreographer Michel Fokine. Since purchasing the school in 1979, Julia Dubno, a Juilliard dance department graduate, has built it into one of New York's leading children's ballet schools, with close to 900 pupils. Faculty includes choreographer Francis Patrelle, who often features students in productions by his company, Dances Patrelle. Though fun, classes are serious and a number of alumni have moved on to the School of American Ballet. Classes, including boy's class, jazz, and tap, are held in two immaculate white studios with windows, mirrors, and, unfortunately, columns. The school has also annexed two additional studios and will eventually have a small Capezio shop on campus.

BALLET HISPANICO SCHOOL OF DANCE

167 W. 89th St.; (212) 362-6710

Begun in 1970 to train dancers for Ballet Hispanico, the Ballet Hispanico School of Dance offers kids ages four to 19 a curriculum strong in classical ballet and traditional Spanish dance. Faculty includes specialists in flamenco, classical and regional Spanish dance, ballet, and children's movement. Classes, held in the company's four spacious studios, are taught to live piano, guitar, or percussion. The school has a high minority enrollment (about 75 percent) and offers scholarships. Performance opportunities abound. Besides the annual spring showcase, open to students of all levels, the most talented advanced level students are eligible for the Ballet Hispanico Student Company, which performs at community gatherings.

BALLET SCHOOL NY

30 E. 31st St.; (212) 679-0401

Diana Byer opened Ballet School NY in 1978, the year after she formed her company, the New York Theater Ballet. In one well-lit studio outfitted with dark wood wainscotting and a wall of mirrors, the school offers ballet classes for adults and children. Children's classes range from pre-ballet (ages three to seven) through an advanced invitation-only class. Former ballet mistress Margaret Craske, who danced with Diaghilev's Ballets Russe, drew up the school's Cecchetti syllabus. Current faculty includes Byer, an alum of Les Grandes Ballets Canadien, Sallie Wilson, a former principal dancer with American Ballet Theater, and assorted company members. Children can dance in the company's annual production of *The Nutcracker* as well as other works. The company also offers a scholarship program for homeless children.

BROADWAY DANCE CENTER
1733 Broadway; (212) 582-9304
This enormous studio's Children's Division offers both serious, pre-professional study and fun classes to develop discipline and confidence. In true megastudio fashion, a variety of disciplines are offered, and students are encouraged to dip into all. The intensive Saturday Program, which requires a placement audition, features five levels of study in ballet, tap, and jazz with additional master classes in African, modern, or theater dance. Weekday open classes in ballet, tap, jazz, and creative movement don't require an audition. There's also a parent–and–child class for wee ones, ages two to three-and-a-half.

BRONX DANCE THEATER
286 E. 204th St., Bronx; (718) 652-7655
In business since 1976, the Bronx Dance Theater, housed in a renovated 1927 movie theater, offers ballet classes for children beginning at age three. The school also provides children's classes in jazz, tap, and modern dance. Besides artistic director Barbara Klein, faculty members include tap teacher Jeff Edmond and ballet teacher Nadine Ilier. Classes

are held in two large, mirrored studios with suspended wood floors. Top students can audition for roles in the Bronx Dance Theater's annual production of *The Nutcracker*.

DISCOVERY PROGRAMS
251 W. 100th St.; (212) 348-5371
424 E. 89th St.; (212) 749-8717
Discovery specializes in recreational ballet for small children, starting with a pre-ballet class for two-year-olds accompanied by an adult. Begun in 1971, the program teaches children basic technique, movement and music appreciation. There's also tap for seven- to 11-year-olds and ballet for eight- to 11-year-olds. Though several serious students have gone on to the School of American Ballet, the emphasis is on fun.

DJONIBA DANCE AND DRUM CENTER
37 E. 18th St.; (212) 477-3464
Djoniba offers a wide range of classes for children ages three to 16. Besides ballet, wee ones can enroll in African dance. For older children, options include ballet, jazz, hip-hop, and African dance and drum classes.

ISADORA DUNCAN FOUNDATION
FOR CONTEMPORARY DANCE
141 W. 26th St.; (212) 691-5040
The Isadora Duncan Foundation holds two classes a week in Duncan technique for children ages nine to 12. Classes are taught in the foundation's airy studio overlooking a terrace. Children under nine must audition; it's best if younger children have already taken dance classes.

FARETA SCHOOL OF DANCE & DRUM
622 Broadway; (212) 677-6708

Fareta, an ethnic dance megastudio, offers classes in African dance for children, ages three to 17.

DONNY GOLDEN SCHOOL OF IRISH DANCE
(718) 238-9207

Irish stepdancer Donny Golden teaches traditional Irish dances to children in after school programs in Brooklyn, the Bronx, and Mineola, Long Island. He starts young children with light reels and easy jigs, danced in soft shoes. They eventually progress to hard-shoe dances, the complex foot patterns that were a precursor of tap dance. Golden, who won a slew of medals in stepdancing competitions, has coached numerous youthful champs, including winners at the New York Regional Championships, held Thanksgiving weekend at the Marriott Hotel in Tarrytown.

MARTHA GRAHAM SCHOOL OF CONTEMPORARY DANCE
316 E. 63d St.; (212) 832-9166

On Saturdays, the Martha Graham School offers classes for teens and for children ages eight to 11. Teens can take Graham technique on a variety of levels, beginning through advanced. Classes in repertory and composition are also available. The children's classes in the fundamentals of the Graham technique are graded by level and/or age. Classes take place in the school's airy white studios, home to the Graham company since the mid 1950s.

ERICK HAWKINS SCHOOL OF DANCE
375 West Broadway; (212) 226-5363
The Hawkins school, best known for adult classes in the so-called freeform technique of founder Erick Hawkins, offers a basic movement class for preschool children.

JOFFREY BALLET SCHOOL/AMERICAN BALLET CENTER
434 Sixth Avenue; (212) 254-8520
The newly christened Joffrey Ballet of Chicago may have fled New York, but its two-story school is still a welcome Village fixture. Classes for kids are serious and systematic. Four- and five-year-olds learn concepts of basic movement and music and get a taste of ballet–class discipline. Pre-ballet classes, ages six to eight, emphasize posture, stretching, and self-discipline. Graded ballet classes follow, along with point and men's class. Former dancers with the Joffrey, New York City Ballet, and similar companies make up the 11-member faculty. The serious study pays off; graduates have gone on to a variety of companies, including the Joffrey. Classes take place in the Joffrey's five upstairs studios equipped with mirrors, windows, white walls, and grand pianos.

THE MANHATTAN BALLET SCHOOL
1556 Third Ave.; (212) 369-3369
Begun over 30 years ago by director Elfriede Merman, the Manhattan Ballet School has turned out generations of well-trained dancers on the Upper East Side. Students usually hear about the school through word of mouth; the landmark building has no sign. The school, which teaches classical ballet exclusively, consists of one large fifth-floor studio. Students, all girls, can enroll in creative movement at age four and begin ballet at eight. Graded classes follow. Talented teens appear in the spring and Christmas productions of the Manhattan Ballet Company.

LUCY MOSES SCHOOL FOR MUSIC AND DANCE
129 W. 67th St.; (212) 362-8060

Music is the main emphasis at the Lucy Moses school, but a small dance program is available for children, ages two through 18. The littlest paricipants start with a hop, skip, and dance class with an adult partner, then move on to pre-ballet and primary ballet. Graded ballet classes follow through intermediate and advanced levels. Classes in jazz, theater dance, and Alexander technique are offered as well. There's also a school performance company.

NATIONAL DANCE INSTITUTE
594 Broadway; (212) 226-0083

Founded by former New York City Ballet dancer Jacques d'Amboise, this 20-year-old program brings dance education to a mix of 15 New York City schools, both public and pirvate. The 30-week program, for fourth, fifth, or sixth graders, reaches 1,500 children, teaching the structure of dance, choreography, and the art of storytelling through dance, music, costumes, and sets. Schools range from PS 1 in China-town to Trinity on the Upper West Side.

NEUBERT BALLET INSTITUTE
881 Seventh Ave.; (212) 246-3166

This serious school, with a nest of elegant skylit studios in Carnegie Hall, offers a children's ballet program and jazz courses for teens.

THE NEW BALLET SCHOOL
890 Broadway; (212) 777-7710

In 1977, Eliot Feld, artistic director of Feld Ballets/NY, founded The New Ballet School to provide tuition-free professional ballet training to New York City public school children with an interest in and facility for dancing. Since then, the school has grown to its current enrollment of some 1,260 kids, all bused to classes in the school's airy downtown headquarters. Working with the New York City Board of Education, the school auditions some 70,000 children in 380 elementary schools each year for approximately 1,000 beginner places. Over 200 students continue each year as intermediate and advanced pupils. The school's primary purpose is to train professional dancers—Darren Gibson, a dynamic principal dancer with Feld Ballets/NY, is its most illustrious grad. But less talented students, it's hoped, learn self-discipline, concentration, and to love dance.

NEW YORK SCHOOL OF CLASSICAL DANCE
944 Eighth Ave.; (212) 397-4852
This ambitious new school, opened in 1992 by artistic director Janet L. Springer, launches eight-year-olds into a rigorous eight-year program of classical ballet training that includes point work and boys' classes. The eight-year-olds take ballet class five times a week. At age nine-and-a-half, students take class at least six days a week. The ultimate goal is to place students in professional ballet and modern companies and win competitions. The school also offers summer ballet intensives with additional training in baroque dance, character dance, and flamenco. Pedagogical classes for instructors are offered as well. Classes are held in the school's mirrored midtown studio, above McDonald's.

92nd STREET Y HARKNESS DANCE CENTER
1395 Lexington Ave.; (212) 415-5552
The Y is a megastudio of sorts for kids with all levels of classes in modern dance, jazz/hip-hop, Isadora Duncan technique, tap, creative dance for ages three to 11, and a serious ballet program through the Harkness Foundation (the foundation moved to the Y after Harkness

House closed in 1985). Bonus: professional choreographers who use the Y's handsome studios often visit the children's classrooms.

PERICHILD

132 Fourth Ave.; (212) 505-0886

The Perichild program, begun in 1986 at the downtown studios of Perry Dance II, enrolls over 250 students in classes for children ages two to 16. Tiny dancers graduate from toddler dancing to creative movement, then start ballet at age five. Graded classes through advanced follow. Other offerings include several levels of hip-hop, tap, jazz, modern dance, ballroom dancing, and tae kwon do. Classes get serious as students progress, and a number of students have graduated to professional careers in dance. Besides five studios, the school has a play area with toys and books.

ROLLER RINKS AT CHELSEA PIERS

23rd St. & the Hudson River; (212) 336-6200

Kids who plan to dance on in-line skates when they grow up can take beginner lessons at the new Roller Rinks at Chelsea Piers. Kids Basic, for ages four to 12, offers simple instruction in five levels. Kids Only Street, for skaters under 18, teaches more aggressive moves.

SCHOOL OF AMERICAN BALLET

70 Lincoln Center Plaza; (212) 877-0600

Started by George Balanchine and Lincoln Kirstein in 1934, this is the gold standard of classical ballet schools, arguably the best in the country. Admission, by audition, is extremely selective. Students from the world over compete for around 300 places. Recreational ballet students need not apply; the school's aim is to train professional dancers. And acceptance is no guarantee of graduation. Once enrolled, students are re-evaluated before they advance from level to level. Most beginners arrive between ages eight and 12, and the rawest start out with a minimum of two classes a week. Intermediate students sign on for a minimum of four classes a week and advanced students must take at least ten classes a week. Though rigorous, class offerings are varied—besides ballet technique, variations, adagio, point, and men's classes, courses include music, gymnastics, ballroom dancing, character dancing, and mime. The faculty, not surprisingly, is superb, with instantly recognizable dance world names like Adam Luders, Suki Schorer, and Stanley Williams. And since 1991, when the school moved into the new Rose Building in Lincoln Center, facilities have been equally top-notch, with five spacious studios, music and physical therapy rooms, and a dorm shared with Juilliard.

SCHOOL OF DANCE THEATER OF HARLEM
466 W. 152d St.; (212) 690-2800
From its inception in a humble Harlem garage in 1968, the School of Dance Theater of Harlem grew prodigiously, moved several times, and finally landed in a smartly renovated three-story building on West 152nd Street with four spacious studios, a library, and a boutique. Attention is lavished on the school's day students, who range from pre-dance three-year-olds to older students and professionals who take serious ballet classes, taught by company members and a range of dance professionals. At present, over 1,300 students attend. Besides ballet, classes are offered in jazz, tap, and ethnic dance—as well as mime, Petipa variations, Dunham technique, and ballroom dance. Top students can perform with the School Ensemble, which presents lecture demonstrations at churches and festivals. A number of graduates dance with Dance Theater of Harlem and other companies.

SOUNDANCE STUDIO

385 Broadway; (212) 941-6457

In autumn 1995, Soundance Studio started a children's program, with creative movement for ages three to five and jazz/modern classes for ages five to ten. Classes in the latter get more technical as the child grows.

SPOKE THE HUB DANCING

748 Union St., Brooklyn; (718) 857-5158

Spoke the Hub offers a wide-ranging children's program, from song, dance and make–believe (ages two to five) to graded ballet classes. Other classes include creative dance, modern dance (age seven and up), African dance, and the dance of Isadora Duncan for wee ones.

STATEN ISLAND BALLET SCHOOL

2205 Richmond Road., Staten Island; (718) 980-0500

Opened in 1993, the new Staten Island Ballet School, official school of the Staten Island Ballet, occupies two refurbished studios in what was once the New Dorp Moravian Church gym. Students currently number around 100, from three-year-olds to teens. Director Ellen Tharp doesn't believe in children's recitals, but students are encouraged to audition for Staten Island Ballet productions that require children, including *The Nutcracker*.

STEPS ON BROADWAY

2121 Broadway; (212) 874-2410

Steps offers a rigorous dance program for children, and in megastudio style, has a faculty of at least seven devoted solely to dancing kids, ages four to 18.

∼ DANCE CAMPS ∼

BRANT LAKE CAMP

Route 8, Brant Lake, New York; (518) 494-2406 or (212) 734-6216

A boy's camp since 1916, Brant Lake is an attractive camp in the piney Adirondacks that also offers a dance and tennis program for girls ages 12 to 16 each summer. Girls can take up to five hours of dance a day (choices include ballet, point, modern, jazz, and tap) or mix dance studies with aerobics, water sports, gymnastics, photography, painting, crafts, and horseback riding. Headed by Sharon Gersten Luckman, an administrator with the Alvin Ailey American Dance Theater, the program also includes a weekly evening visit to performances of New York City Ballet, the Philadelphia Orchestra, or a rock concert at the narby Saratoga Performing Arts Center.

CHAUTAUQUA DANCE

Chautauqua Institute Schools Office, Box 1098,
Chautauqua, New York 14722; (716) 357-6233 or 357-6234

Jean-Pierre Bonnefous, a former principal dancer with New York City Ballet, heads this summer ballet program for girls and boys near the grounds of the famous Chautauqua summer festival in southwest New ʟork State. The serious program, open to girls 11 through 17 and boys 14 through 18, includes study with the eight-member faculty, master classes with guest faculty members like Violette Verdy, Patricia McBride, John Clifford, and Lynne Taylor Corbett, and lectures on topics like dance medicine and nutrition. Core classes include technique, point, partnering, and flamenco. Jazz and modern dance classes are offered as well. Bonus: students can attend any Chautauqua Festival concerts, plays, films, opera, and art exhibitions they please.

USDAN CENTER FOR THE CREATIVE & PERFORMING ARTS

Huntington, Long Island; (212) 772-6060 or (516) 724-0136

Usdan is the ultimate day camp for kids fascinated by the arts. Held June through August in a Huntington forest outfitted with 70 wood-frame studios, the camp offers programs in music, art, theater arts, creative writing, and, of course, dance for boys and girls ages eight through 18. Students major in one art, minor in another, and swim for an hour each day. Though some campers are aspiring performers, talent is not an admission requirement. But programs are top-notch, taught by professionals in each field, mostly from New York. Classes are offered in ballet, modern, jazz, tap, and folk dance.

∽ SCHOLARSHIPS ∽

The following is a sampling of schools that offer financial aid, including full and partial scholarships. An audition is usually required.

Alvin Ailey American Dance Center

Ballet Academy East

Ballet Hispanico

Ballet School NY

Bronx Dance Theater

Chautauqua Dance

Joffrey Ballet School (for trainee students only)

The New Ballet School (tuition-free instruction
   for New York City public school kids)

New Dance Group

School of American Ballet

School of the Dance Theater of Harlem

Steps on Broadway

~ **CHAPTER FIVE** ~

Dance Academics

DANCING AND HITTING THE BOOKS may seem like polar opposites, but dance has its cerebral, scholarly side. Like art and music, dance comes with a rich history you can study in a classroom. And you don't have to pull on tights and stand at a barre to dissect subjects like music theory and notation.

It's no surprise that New York City, home to every dance class imaginable, is also a center for academic dance. Metropolitan New York is dotted with colleges and universities offering some of the most sophisticated and successful dance programs in the country. You can sign on for a full undergraduate or graduate course load and emerge as a professional dancer, a dance instructor, an arts administrator, or a movement therapist. Or you can audit courses here and there and get a lot more out of your next visit to the New York City Ballet.

The city also is well stocked with small, specialized schools, like the Laban/Bartenieff Institute of Movement Studies. And for a painless dose of action *and* academia, the New School's studio classes in subjects like classical ballet and flamenco are supplemented with classroom discussions of history and theory and, for the intrepid, serious reading lists.

～ NEW YORK SCHOOLS, COLLEGES ～ AND UNIVERSITIES

BARNARD COLLEGE/COLUMBIA UNIVERSITY
3009 Broadway; (212) 854-2995

Dance is integrated into a liberal arts curriculum at Barnard. Besides performance and choreographic skills, the program emphasizes dance's place in history and culture. Class offerings include kinesiology, movement analysis, dance history, and dance criticism as well as studio classes in ballet, modern, jazz, character, Spanish, and musical theater dance. Guest lecturers in choreography have included New York City Ballet's Robert LaFosse, Sean Lavery, and Alexandre Proia, among others.

CITY COLLEGE OF NEW YORK
Amsterdam Ave. at 140th St.; (212) 650-6635

Besides technique classes in ballet, modern, jazz, and African dance, CCNY offers courses in composition, dance notation, dance history, anatomy, music for dancers, and improvisation. The most promising students are invited to become members of Citidance, the student company, which performs on campus at Aaron Davis Hall. The large faculty includes Carolyn Adams, Deborah Carr, and critic Robert Greskovic, among others.

DANCE NOTATION BUREAU
31 W. 21st St.; (212) 807-7899

Since 1940, the Dance Notation Bureau has served as a repository for dances preserved by Labanotation, Rudolf Laban's widely used system for recording movement. The bureau's archives currently house over 460 dance scores by more than 160 of the world's preeminent choreographers, including George Balanchine, Paul Taylor, and Antony Tudor. Besides assisting in stagings and maintaining a library, the bureau offers correspondence courses in Labanotation theory. Though many colleges teach Labanotation, only the bureau offers professional notator certification.

HUNTER COLLEGE, THE CITY UNIVERSITY OF NEW YORK
695 Park Ave.; (212) 772-5012

With a superb Upper East Side location, Hunter College is well stocked with classrooms and rather austere, business-like practice studios, which New York dance companies often rent. Courses are offered in ballet, modern, jazz, folk, and ethnic dance as well as dance history, anatomy/kinesiology, composition, improvisation, music for dance, dance instruction, and production.

THE JUILLIARD SCHOOL
60 Lincoln Plaza; (212) 799-5000

Doris Humphrey was instrumental in establishing the dance department at Juilliard and today the school's rigorous four-year undergraduate program is for aspiring professional ballet and modern dancers. The faculty includes Paul Taylor alums Carolyn Adams and

Linda Kent as well as Bessie Schönberg, the brilliant composition teacher. The numerous dance offerings include studio classes in ballet, modern, partnering, point, jazz, tap, and Alexander technique

LABAN BARTENIEFF INSTITUTE OF MOVEMENT STUDIES
11 E. 4th St.; (212) 477-4299

The institute is headquarters for the development and study of the movement principles devised by Rudolf Laban and developed further by his student Irmgard Bartenieff. Laban Movement Analysis provides a language for looking at, describing, and analyzing movement. Bartenieff fundamentals synthesize Laban's theories and apply them to the body. The institute offers a certification program and a slew of special programs, including courses in dance movement therapy, anatomy and kinesiology, and kinespherics. Classes in dance and holistic aerobics are offered as well.

MARYMOUNT MANHATTAN COLLEGE
221 E. 71st St.; (212) 517-0651

Dance courses at Marymount Manhattan fall into two categories—one for aspiring professional ballet or modern dancers and the other for students who plan to teach. Students in both programs take technique and music classes. Course offerings include ballet, jazz and modern dance, choreography, dance history, rhythmic training, music for dance, and techniques of teaching.

THE NEW SCHOOL FOR SOCIAL RESEARCH
66 W. 21st St.; (212) 229-5762

With three departments specializing in movement—dance, recreation, and fitness—the New School offers a huge selection of classes that neatly blend academic instruction with active movement. Teachers discuss the subject—be it the history of ballet or the origins of flamenco—then students receive technique instruction in one of the school's spacious studios. Students enrolled in longer courses also receive bibliographies so they can pursue additional work on their own. Recent offerings have included country and western, cajun, flamenco, ballet/modern, classical ballet, t'ai chi/modern, Afro-Brazilian, jazz, hip-hop, and ballroom, as well as Alexander technique, ice dancing, and Bartenieff fundamentals of Laban Movement Analysis for aching backs.

NEW YORK UNIVERSITY, SCHOOL OF EDUCATION
675 Education Building, Washington Square; (212) 998-5400
The Dance Division of New York University's School of Education trains dance instructors. Undergrads work toward certification as dance teachers for kindergarten through 12th grade or teaching positions in professional studios, while graduate students prepare for careers in dance administration or teaching dance in higher education. Courses include technique classes in ballet, modern, jazz, and ethnic-folk dance as well as courses in music theory, criticism, movement sciences, composition, notation, stagecraft-production, history, teaching methods, and the aesthetics of dance.

NEW YORK UNIVERSITY, TISCH SCHOOL OF THE ARTS
111 Second Ave.; (212) 998-1980
New York University's Tisch School specializes in professional training in dance and choreography. The facilities include five studios and theaters for the 14 to 16 concerts presented each year. Class offerings include technical training in ballet, contemporary and men's dance, partnering, and point as well as composition, criticism, dance history, movement, music theory, and improvisation.

PERRY DANCE II

132 Fourth Ave.; (212) 505-0886

Ilana Suprun, a former soloist and choreologist with Israel's Bat-Dor Dance Company, teaches Benesh Notation at Perry Dance II. Though less popular in the U.S. than Labanotation, Benesh is widely used overseas, notably by London's Royal Ballet.

∼ WESTCHESTER COUNTY ∼

BARD COLLEGE

Annandale-on-Hudson; (914) 758-6822

Among the dance offerings at Bard are ballet, five types of modern dance, flamenco, and Afro-Cuban. Courses are available in composition, anatomy, music for dancers, and dance history. Choreography and performance are emphasized.

PURCHASE COLLEGE, THE STATE UNIVERSITY OF NEW YORK

735 Anderson Hill Road, Purchase; (914) 251-6800

The dance building at Purchase College is a student's dream come true, with glass walls, spacious studios with pianos, and classrooms galore. The program, with its emphasis on performance and choreography for ballet and modern dance, is also top-notch, with courses in music, dance history, and more. Students wishing to perform can audition for the Purchase Dance Corps., which tours with a repertory of works by George Balanchine, Merce Cuningham, Doris Humphrey, Mark Morris, and Paul Taylor as well as new works by guest choreographers and faculty members.

SARAH LAWRENCE COLLEGE
One Mead Way, Bronxville; (914) 395-2433
Forty percent of Sarah Lawrence's undergrads specialize in the performing arts. Not surprisingly, the dance program, based on modern technique, is aimed toward performance (alumni include Lucinda Childs, Meredith Monk, Carolyn Adams, and Maia Garrison of Urban Bush Women). Besides five technique classes a week, students can study composition, improvisation, Labanotation, ballet, anatomy, dance history, and music.

$\sim$ LONG ISLAND $\sim$

ADELPHI UNIVERSITY
Garden City; (516) 877-4250
Contemporary dance pioneer Ruth St. Denis began Adelphi's dance program in 1938. Besides courses in ballet and modern techniques, classes are offered in composition, dance history, dance theory, and the principles of teaching dance.

$\sim$ CONNECTICUT $\sim$

CONNECTICUT COLLEGE
270 Mohegan Avenue, New London; (860) 439-2830
Connecticut College's dance department has a long, distinguished history. The American Dance Festival, now held in Durham, North Carolina, originated here, and countless modern dance titans, like José Limón and Doris Humphrey, spent time on the campus. These days, emphasis is on performing, choreographing, teaching, dance administration, and fitness. Courses include dance history, music for dance, movement analysis, and sport/dance medicine.

TRINITY COLLEGE

Department of Theater and Dance, Hartford; (860) 297-2330

Trinity's dance program is linked with the school's drama program and emphasizes performance and technical and historical aspects of dance. Besides courses in ballet, modern, African, and jazz technique, classes include dance history, dancing and music, and women in theater and dance. In addition, students can take an intensive semester of theater-dance study in New York at LaMama Theater.

WESLEYAN UNIVERSITY

Middletown; (860) 685-2290

Wesleyan offers an undergraduate dance program and a graduate program in movement studies. Courses include dance technique (modern, ballet, jazz, tap, African, Javanese, South Indian), improv, composition, choreography, performance, history, ethnology, and teaching methods.

～ NEW JERSEY ～

MONTCLAIR STATE UNIVERSITY

Upper Montclair; (201) 655-7080

For students wishing to perform, Montclair State has a wealth of resources, including a 1,000-seat theater, two experimental theaters, two dance studios, and a television studio. Dance courses include ballet, jazz and modern dance, rhythmic analysis, and Labanotation.

RUTGERS, THE STATE UNIVERSITY OF NEW JERSEY

P.O. Box 270, New Brunswick; (908) 932-8497

The dance program at Rutgers is geared toward professional dance; three graduates from 1993 are current members of the Nikolais and Murray Louis Dance Theater. Besides technique classes in ballet, modern, jazz and ethnic dance, courses include improvisation, choreography, dance notation, Laban Movement Analysis.

CHAPTER SIX

Gotta Dance

YOU'VE TAKEN LESSONS, you've watched performances, now you want to do it yourself, be it the Argentine tango, Balkan folk dances, or the hottest hip-hop steps. Fortunately, New York is bulging with havens specializing in all the above and much more, from dancing on in-line skates to Texas two-stepping on a Saturday night. There's even a club where tappers can hop on stage and improvise, provided they're good.

Besides offering a welcome place to indulge in aerobic exercise and show off what you're learned, New York's participatory dance spots are terrific places to meet people, be it future spouses or just fellow dance aficionados. Some of the best dances, after all, are social. The following is a hint of the vast assortment of places to go dancing.

∼ BALLROOM/LATIN ∼

CLUB BROADWAY
2700 Queens Plaza South, Long Island City; (718) 937-7111
Dress up for Latin dancing, with a big dose of salsa, Thursday through Saturday nights, plus the last Sunday of the month.

COPACABANA
617 W. 57th St.; (212) 582-2672
Dance to live Latin and disco music Tuesdays, Fridays, and Saturdays.

HIDEAWAY
32 W. 37th St.; (212) 947-8940
The dance floor at this midtown restaurant is snug but that hardly bothers couples who happily dance to live Latin and ballroom music, Mondays through Saturdays.

LATIN QUARTER
2551 Broadway; (212) 864-7600
Formerly Club Broadway, this Upper West Side club has benefited handsomely from its recent facelift, which included a much-needed air-conditioning system. Latin enthusiasts consider it one of the best dance spots in town.

MARC BALLROOM
27 Union Square West; (212) 867-3789
On alternate Sunday evenings this spacious basement, with an entrance next to the hip Coffee Shop restaurant, turns into a ballroom, 7 p.m. to midnight. The room, a one-time union hall, isn't naturally atmospheric, but when the lights dim and the music swells, over 200 people swing and sway their hearts out. Veteran Roseland DJ Sammy Philips spins tapes— cha chas, mambos, salsas, the hustle, foxtrots, the peabody. Fee: $10.

THE RAINBOW ROOM
30 Rockefeller Center; (212) 632-5100
The Art Deco palace in the sky presents ballroom and Latin dancing to the Rainbow Room Orchestra Tuesday to Saturday, 7:30 p.m. to 1 a.m., Sundays 6 to 11 p.m. Fee: $20 after 11 p.m.

ROSELAND
239 W. 52nd St.; (212) 247-0200
Manhattan's legendary midtown ballroom, in somewhat inelegant decline, throws open its big glass doors Sundays and Thursdays for ballroom dancing, 2 p.m. to 11 p.m. Dance to a live band on Sundays, famed dance DJ Sammy Philips's hand picked sounds on Thursdays. Music is strictly ballroom, American and Latin. Fees: Sundays, $11; Thursday, $7.

SATURDAY NIGHT BALLROOM AT THE 92ND STREET Y
Lexington Ave. at 92nd Street; (212) 996-1100
Saturday Night Ballroom has become a tradition at the Y, with 7 p.m. lessons taught by instructors from the Sandra Cameron Dance Center,

followed by dancing 8 p.m. to midnight. Swings, waltzes, tangos, mambos—everything is taught and danced. Call for precise nights. Fee: $12.

S.O.B.'S
204 Varick St.; (212) 243-4940

Dance to live Latin, Caribbean, or soul music at S.O.B.'s, a.k.a. Sounds of Brazil, almost every night. And learn to dance on Mondays. A different strain of Latin dance—mambo/salsa, merengue, Afro-Cuban— is taught each week, 7 p.m. to 8 p.m. Music by top Latin orchestras follow, and dancers can stick around at no extra charge. Fee: $8.

THE SUPPER CLUB
240 W. 47th St.; (212) 921-1940

The Barry Levitt Orchestra plays for ballroom enthusiasts Friday and Saturday nights at this theater–district dinner club. Dance to recorded music Monday nights, 8 p.m. to 1 a.m.

∼ SWING ∼

MIDSUMMER NIGHT SWING
Lincoln Center; (212) 875-5102

For 20 nights each summer hundreds of dancers swing, tango, and waltz the evening away at Lincoln Center's Fountain Plaza, Wednesdays though Saturdays. Each night means a different style of dance with a live band—international ballroom, 1950s rhythm & blues, mambo and merengue, tango, country and western, Vienna waltz, West Coast swing. An hour of lessons start the proceedings Wednesdays through Fridays, followed by nearly three hours of dancing. Fee: $8

THE NEW YORK SWING DANCE SOCIETY

P.O. Box 1512, New York 10009; (212) 696-9737

When the old Savoy Ballroom in Harlem closed, big band swing dance enthusiasts created the Swing Dance Society. The organization, which lives to promote swing, is famed for its Savoy Sunday Big Band Dances in Union Square at Irving Plaza, 17 Irving Place. Doors open at 7 p.m., a live band starts playing at 8, and members and nonmembers jive until midnight. Free 7 p.m. dance lessons are offered weekly in July and August, monthly the rest of the year. The crowd is mixed, ages 25 to 85; partners aren't a must since people partner up on the floor. The Lindy hop, so named after Charles Lindbergh's solo hop across the Atlantic in 1927, evolved into swing in 1935, when the Swing Era officially began. Its fame spread with a group of Savoy dancers, called Whitey's Lindy Hoppers, who performed in movies and musicals. For a touch of authenticity, Frankie Manning, an original member of Whitey's, shows up here frequently, leading crowds in the Shim Sham, a popular line dance. Fees: nonmembers, $12; members, $8; dues are $35 a year.

NORTH RIVER BAR

145 Hudson St.; (212) 226-9411

This Tribeca bar offers West Coast swing to recorded music, Tuesdays at 9 p.m. Fee: $6

NOTE: *The Ballroom Review* is a terrific guide to ballroom, Latin, and swing events in the New York area featuring places to dance, interviews with dance teachers, reviews, and other news and information. Annual subscription: $26. Write to 60 Gramercy Park North, New York 10010.

∼ CLASSIC BALLROOM ∼

VINTAGE DANCE SOCIETY

Book-Friends Cafe, 16 W. 18th St.; (212) 255-7407

The waltz, schottische, and turkey trot are a few of the historic dances performed alternate Friday nights, September to June, at Manhattan's Book-Friends Cafe (the dance floor becomes surprisingly spacious once they shove aside the book shelves). Sponsored by the Connecticut-based Vintage Dance Society, which preserves and reconstructs music and dance from 1840 to 1925, sessions include dances from the Civil War to the speakeasy era, with appropriate taped music. Musical evolution, from the waltz to Scott Joplin rags, helped shape these dances as did changes in social mores and even clothing. "Women wearing corsets danced differently from women not wearing corsets," says society founder Marc Casslar. Evenings start with a demonstration and lesson, followed by social dancing. Dancers change partners frequently, since that's how it was done 100 years ago—and it's an easy way to bring newcomers up to speed. The society also sponsors fancy dress balls, tango soirees, and similar events where white tie doesn't look weird. Fee: $6; dinner additional.

∼ TAP ∼

DEANNA'S

130 E. 7th St.; (212) 505-5288

Sunday night is tap night starting at 10 p.m. at this tiny downtown club. There's a band, and tappers Max Pollak and Herbin van Cayselle oversee the proceedings, inviting appropriately shoed audience members onto Deanna's compact stage for percussive improv. "It's always people who know how to tap," Pollak says. The result is a delicious range of styles, from rhythm to Broadway, with lots of solos. "There's not much room," Pollak admits.

LA PLACE ON THE PARK
308 W. 58th St.; (212) 664-1308

Tappers call it Hoofer's Night. One Thursday a month, tip-top tappers turn up at La Place and improvise, led by master tapper Jimmy Slyde. "He moves like butter on a hot stove," says tapper Mark Goodman admiringly. Other regulars include Herbin van Layselle and Savion Glover, though not knowing who to expect is half the fun. As many as a dozen dancers tap away, first solo, then in groups. It's jazzy improv at its best. The audience is filled with tappers, too. Fee: $10 cover, $10 minimum

∼ HIP-HOP, HOUSE, AND THEME DANCING ∼

LIMELIGHT
Avenue of the Americas at 20th Street; (212) 807-7850

This big desanctified Chelsea church with atmospheric stained glass windows and spiral staircases offers themed music, dancing, and nightclubbing Tuesdays through Sundays, 10 p.m. to 4 a.m. Dance to house music Thursday through Saturday, rock & roll on Sundays, and alternative on Tuesdays. Also watch for novelties, like the foam dancing craze of summer 1995.

PALLADIUM
126 E. 14th St.; (212) 473-7171

Another Über club, open Thursday through Sunday, 10 p.m. to 5 a.m., with house, hip-hop, and reggae music. Expect big-club fads, like foam dancing.

SOUND FACTORY
12 W. 21st St.; (212) 206-0600
Look for the most cutting-edge house and hip-hop dancing in town on
Wednesday nights.

∼ FOLK/COUNTRY ∼

BALKAN DANCES
Hungarian House, 213 E. 82d St.;
(212) 942-3768 or (212) 249-9360
Balkan dance enthusiasts gather at Hungarian House on Friday nights,
mid-September through mid-June, to perform the popular line dances
of Romania, Greece, Bulgaria, Turkey, and the former Yugoslav
republics (Hungarian and Western European dances are tossed in, too,
occasionally). Though taped music is the norm, live musicians and
guest teachers show up for a monthly special–events night. Newcomers
are welcome, but organizer David Ginsberg, a top Balkan dance
teacher, suggests they call first or write for a schedule.

COUNTRY DANCE NEW YORK
P.O. Box 878, Village Station, New York 10011; (212) 459-4080
This large, active organization sponsors traditional social dances
featuring English country and American contra dances. The two dance
styles—lines of men and women negotiating complex steps and
figures—stretch back to both 17th-century England and America's 13
colonies. "Thomas Jefferson would recognize some of these dances,"
says enthusiast David Simonoff. English country dances stick close to
the music; American contra dances are a bit more freeform. Contra
dancers meet Saturday nights and country dancers Tuesday nights at
the Metropolitan Duane United Methodist Church, 201 West 13th

Street at Seventh Avenue, September to May. Dances feature callers, refreshments, live music, and a teaching session, so newcomers are as welcome as pros. During summers, the group meets in parks. CDNY also organizes special events, including balls and parties. Fees: contra dances, $7 for CDNY members, $9 nonmembers; country dances, $7 members, $8 nonmembers; annual membership dues, $15.

IRISH TRADITIONAL DANCING

Irish American Center, 297 Willis Ave., Mineola; (516) 746-9392

Denis O'Sullivan leads classic Irish ceili dances—sets, jigs, reels—on Wednesday evenings, year 'round except August, at Mineola's spacious Irish American Center. After a round of lessons starting around 7:30 p.m., the serious group dancing begins and lasts "until everyone gets tired," a regular happily reports. The center also sponsors monthly ceili dances, sans lessons, with a caller and a band (fiddle, accordian, drum). Fees: lesson/dances, $3; dances, $7.

ISRAELI FOLK DANCE

92nd Street Y, 92nd St. and Lexington Ave.; (212) 415-5737

For more than 30 years, the 92nd Street Y has hosted Israeli folk dancing, currently led by Ruth Goodman and Danny Uziel. After a lesson starting at 6:45 p.m., the serious, high-octane dancing commences at 8 p.m., Wednesday nights in Buttenweiser Hall and Lounge. Look for seasonal specialties, like the Rosh Hashana Marathon and the Winter Warm-up-the-Chills Marathon. Steps are energetic, rhythmic, and enjoyable. Fee: $8.

JAPANESE CLASSICAL AND FOLK DANCING

New York Buddhist Church, 331-332 Riverside Dr.;
(718) 271-7352

Members of the Tachibana Dance Group, trained by Tokyo's prestigious Tachibana Dance School, hold Saturday classes and dance sessions in Japanese folk and classical dance, September through June at New York Buddhist Church. Japanese dance enthusiasts also flock to the annual Obon Festival, a traditional summer dance in a New York park one day each July. Neophytes can avoid embarrassment by signing on for pre-festival practice lessons offered by the church. Fee: $30 a month.

LOUISIANA COMMUNITY BAR AND GRILL

622 Broadway; (212) 460-9633

Sunday night is cajun dancing night at this lively Village bar, with live music.

NEW YORK METROPOLITAN COUNTRY
MUSIC ASSOCIATION

P.O. 201, Bellrose 11426; (718) 763-4328
Glendale Memorial Building, 72nd St. & Myrtle Ave., Queens

Formed around the time John Travolta danced the Texas two-step in *Urban Cowboy*, this enthusiatic group meets Saturday nights at Queens's Glendale Memorial Building for Western dancing: line dancing, freestyle swing, Texas two-step—"the same dances you see on TNN," says president Rich Cohen. A free dance lesson starts at 8:30 p.m., followed by dancing to live music and DJ tapes. Bonus: the association publishes a bimonthly newsletter of local country events. Fees: nonmembers, $8, members, $5; annual membership dues, $18.

ROYAL SCOTTISH COUNTRY DANCE SOCIETY

McBurney YMCA, 215 W. 23rd St.;
(212) 741-9210 or (212) 255-7822

The Scottish country reels, jigs, and strathspeys danced Thursday nights at the McBurney Y are performed the world over by members of the Royal Country Dance Society, an Edinburgh-based organization that standardized Scotland's country dances in the 1920s. Though similar to English country dances, "Scottish dance is very balletic," says Miriam Zwerin, a regular at the dances. Dancers point their toes, turn out their feet and deliberately hit their ankles, making heel-less soft-soled shoes a must. The balletic influence is, in fact, French, dating from the 16th-century Auld Alliance between Scotland and France. Dress code: dancers must wear soft-soled shoes; women should wear skirts. Fees: $7; Royal Society membership dues, $15.

SCANDINAVIAN COUPLE-TURNING DANCES

Town & Village Synagogue, 334 E.14th St.; (212) 758-5542

Wednesday nights, October through June, this downtown synagogue goes Scandinavian, with traditional couple-turning dances from Sweden, Norway, and Denmark, 8 p.m. to 10:30 p.m., preceded by a lesson at 7 p.m. Expect to hear live fiddle music, often on the Norwegian Hardanger fiddle, which looks like a violin with too many strings. Though participants need not be Swedish or seasoned folk dancers, the more enthusiastic members have studied dance in Scandinavia, and, upon request, perform in full costume at local folk festivals. Teachers and musicians from Sweden and Norway occasionally show up for a dose of the real thing. Fee: $7 to $8.

SWEDISH FOLK DANCERS OF NEW YORK

McBurney YMCA, 215 W. 23rd St.;
(212) 741-9210 or (914) 725-3543

Dating from 1903, this is—surprise, surprise—the nation's oldest Swedish folk dance gathering. Dances, Thursday nights from 8 p.m. until the wee hours of 10 or 11 p.m., include traditional Swedish line, couple and circle dances, with a walk-through before each dance. Veterans partner newcomers to speed the learning process. The 16-member core group also performs at Swedish festivals and other events, so call first to make certain they're dancing at the Y. No dances during the summer or holidays. Fee: $2.

∼ SKATES ∼

ROLLER RINKS AT CHELSEA PIERS

Chelsea Piers, 23rd St. and Hudson River; (212) 336-6200

Skaters lace up their boots and dance under the stars on summer Friday and Saturday nights, 8 p.m. to 11 p.m., at Chelsea Pier. DJs spin the latest music. Fee: $8.

ROXY

515 W. 18th St.; (212) 645-5156

This cavernous Chelsea roller rink dims its lights, turns up the house music, and opens its doors to dancing in-line and quad skates, Tuesdays and Wednesdays. Those with tired legs, or squeaky wheels, can rest up on the enormous mohair sofas, ca. 1935, on the sidelines. The atmosphere is highly theatrical and oddly romantic. Tuesday is gay night and Wednesday straight night, though regulars say no one gets too miffed about crosssover skaters. Fee: $12.

CHAPTER SEVEN

Being the Best: Competitive Dance

COMPETITIVE DANCE PROBABLY dates from the first cave dwellers who wanted to see who could kick the highest and spin the fastest. These days, things are more refined—competitive ballroom dancing, after all, will be an exhibition event at the 1996 Summer Olympics. But the urge to be the best dancer on your block, or your planet, is as strong as ever. And for the growing ranks of amateurs and professionals who dance for prizes as well as pleasure, options abound.

Look hard enough, and you'll find an organized competition for nearly every strain of dance, from Irish stepdancing to classical ballet. But most of the attention is lavished on competitive ballroom, with partnering classics like foxtrot, quick step, and waltz as well as Latin turns like cha cha, rumba, and paso doble. Unlike club ballroom, where dancers improvise as they please, competitive dancers must adhere to standardized steps set down by national or international organizations. If you ignore the rules, you won't win, no matter how sensationally you dance.

Two basic styles—international and American—dominate competitive ballroom. International-style dancers, performing moves set by the Imperial Society of Teachers of Dancing in England, are perfect partners, never a step apart. Steps are by the book, literally, and the society's hefty rule books are updated regularly. American style dancing is more reminiscent of Fred and Ginger. Dancers sometimes separate, and the steps, while codified, often evolve from social dancing.

Unfortunately, none of the major competitions takes place in New York. "Too expensive," says Theo Derleth, a partner in the Fred Astaire franchise on the Upper West Side. Competition connoisseurs can make due watching PBS broadcasts of the annual Ohio Star Ballroom competition, a biggie. Or you can travel to one of the major events listed below. And if you yearn to compete, don your marabou boa and sign up with a ballroom school specializing in competitive dance (see Chapter Three). The best place to learn about competitions is from an instructor who's been there—and won.

Dance Competitions

∼ BALLROOM/LATIN ∼

IMPERIAL SOCIETY OF TEACHERS OF DANCING

Britain's Imperial Society oversees several big competitions in the United States each year. Competitions are grand four-day affairs, with between 400 and 500 competitors at all levels, from children ("they're adorable," says society president Lorraine Hahn) up through amateurs, pro-ams (usually dance instructors and students), and professionals.

The Eastern United States Championships, late February or early March, take place in the grand ballroom of Bally's Park Place Casino Hotel and Tower, Park Place and Boardwalk, Atlantic City, New Jersey (609) 340-2000

The North American Championships, which include Canadian competitors, are in July at the Adams Mark Hotel, City Avenue and Monument Road, Philadelphia, Pennsylvania 19131; (215) 581-5000.

And the Imperial Championships, with competitors from all over the world, are also at the Adams Mark Hotel, in December.

UNITED STATES BALLROOM CHAMPIONSHIPS

American Ballroom Competition
P.O. Box 453605, Miami, Florida 33245; (305) 442-1288
One of the biggies, this competitive extravaganza, featuring top dancers from across the country, is held in early September in the Grand Ballroom of Miami's Fountainbleau Hilton Resort.

～ BALLET ～

NEW YORK INTERNATIONAL BALLET COMPETITION
111 W. 57th St., Suite 1400; (212) 956-1520

It may not be as famous as the other big ballet competitions, like the Erik Bruhn or the USA International, but the New York International Ballet Competition, held every three years since 1983, attracts a strong roster of young dancers ages 17 to 24 *and* is held in Manhattan. Slated for Alice Tully Hall, the June 1996 competition is expected to attract dancers from New York as well as Europe, Asia, South America, and the Middle East. Contestants spend three weeks in New York, take daily classes, receive coaching, and participate in the final night's awards ceremony and performance. Dancers, judged on artistry and individual interpretation, perform the pas de deux from *Les Sylphides*, a solo of their choice, and three additional pas de deux. Judges have included Maya Plisetskaya, Alicia Alonso, Violette Verdy, Arthur Mitchell, and Cynthia Gregory. Among recent winners, America's Victoria Mazzorelli currently dances with the Frankfurt Ballet and Cuba's Jose Manuel Carreno is with American Ballet Theater.

~ **CHAPTER EIGHT** ~

Dance Gear and Memorabilia

AS ANYONE KNOWS WHO VISITS MEGASTUDIOS like Steps or watches the leggy ones dashing into the State Theater, dancers have a style all their own. It's not just the turned out feet and erect posture that set them apart. It's the sassy way a ballerina pulls her baseball cap over her ponytail or carelessly wraps a pink practice sweater around her waist. Having a mere 3.5 percent body fat ratio certainly enhances the look as well, but so do the proper clothes, both for street and studio.

As befits an international shopping capital, New York is well stocked with shops that sell nothing but clothing, shoes, and accessories for dancers. The ranks are further swollen by department stores, sock shops, and sports gear outposts that deal in 'tards and tights. But for purists looking for one-stop shopping on a grand scale, from tap shoes to flamenco skirts, Manhattan's dance shops are as good as it gets. New York is also a superb place to find the hottest salsa tape, the juiciest Nureyev biography, and autographed point shoes worn by Maya Plisetskaya or Paloma Herrera.

THE BALLET SHOP

1887 Broadway; (212) 581-7990

The place to go for dance books (hard-to-find and less so), recordings, cassettes of dance scores, VCRs of landmark ballets, and a lively assortment of memorabilia, from ballerina lockets to Gelsey Kirkland's autographed point shoes. All the arcane goodies are sold—classroom music tapes, technique VCRs—as well as countless autographed photographs of dance greats old and young. Best of all is the ambiance, which seems straight out of *The Red Shoes*. The staff is knowledgeable and savvy. And dancers love the place. I once watched a mob of Brazilians eagerly snap photos of Fernando Bujones, who had stopped by the shop and posed good-naturedly. "Does this always happen to you?" I asked him. "Only at the The Ballet Shop," he replied.

CAPEZIO

1650 Broadway; (212) 245-2130
1776 Broadway; (212) 586-5140
136 E. 61st St.; (212) 758-8833
(at Ailey) 211 W. 61st St.; (212) 397-3060
(at Steps) 2121 Broadway; (212) 799-7774

It seems there's a Capezio shop almost everywhere dancers congregate in Manhattan. But the showstoppers are Capezio's enormous megastores on Broadway at 51st and 57th Streets. Both billeted on the second floor, they offer a vast, multicolored selection of leotards, tights, knit legwarmers, practice dresses, jazz shorts, flamenco skirts, workout clothes, sheer ballet skirts, and kiddie wear—sweetly miniature 'tards and tutus. Newest tight: the convertible which can go from footed to footless. Both shops have enormous shoe departments, each featuring Capezio's 11 styles of point shoes, split-sole ballet shoes, jazz shoes, modern dance sandals, tap shoes, even soft Highland ghillies. The 51st Street shop also sells dance videos, and both stock dance magazines and a sprinkling of books. Both stores also have big bulletin boards listing auditions, dance events, classes, and other need-to-know items. Best novelty: the TeleTone tap key chain.

CASA LATINA

151 E. 116th St.; (212) 427-6062

This is arguably the best place in town for the latest Latin dance cassettes and tapes. The stock is dazzling.

COUNTRY DANCE AND SONG SOCIETY

17 New South St., Northampton, Massachusetts 01060;
(413) 584-9913

Founded in 1915, this national association of English and American folk dance and music enthusiasts, 3,000 members strong, sells by mail order hard-to-find books and recordings related to English and American country dance—English country, contra, morris, sword, garland, square, clog, and Irish stepdancing.

DANCE RECORDINGS AND SHOES

230 Seventh Ave.; (212) 691-1934

Opened in 1975 to specialize in hard-to-find international dance recordings, this frill-free upstairs shop has since branched into the dance shoe business as well. Besides American-made ballet and tap shoes like Leo's and La Mendola, the shop carries Irish step-dancing ghillies, flamenco shoes, and a vast collection of ballroom shoes for men and women (one flashy men's pair is smoth-ered in glitter). There's also a large selection of ballroom and ballet CDs and cassettes, and instructional videos for ballet, ballroom, and even folk dancing.

DANSKIN

159 Columbus Ave.

Danskin Inc., makers of tights, leotards and other dance togs, opened this new superstore near Lincoln

Center in November 1995. Besides dancewear by Danskin and Dance France, the shop carries sportswear and workout clothes.

LARRY FARLEY
(212) 595-0074
Larry Farley's charcoal and oil renderings of dancers were a hit when six enormous canvases went on sale in the New York City Ballet's mezzanine boutique during the Spring 1995 season. Farley studied ballet for years but began too late 'to dance professionally. Instead, he channeled his energies into art, painting and drawing dancers he admires in ballets he likes, usually danced by NYCB. Canvases start at $1,000.

FREED OF LONDON
922 Seventh Ave.; (212) 489-1055
This handsome, street-level shop stocks dance clothes and shoes by Freed, the popular English shoemaker, and Chacott, Japan's largest dance shoemaker. Elegant with big mirrors, this civilized shop offers racks of leotards in intriguing color combinations, knit warm-up wear and a large area with benches for trying on shoes. Neatest novelty: toe shoe Christmas tree ornaments in pink or red satin.

THE GALLERY AT LINCOLN CENTER
(212) 580-4673
With its gray walls and sensitive lighting, this inviting concourse-level exhibition space is perfect for a quick visit before catching a performance upstairs. The gallery specializes in performing arts photographs, artwork, and memorabilia, with shows based on companies currently visiting Lincoln Center. During summer performances by the Kirov Ballet, the gallery displayed black–and–white company photographs by Nina Alovert. Shows stay up three weeks to a month.

GLITTER

1733 Broadway; (212) 247-0910

More a shopette than a shop, Glitter specializes in jazzwear—Capezio jazz shoes and skirts, tights, T-shirts, bodysuits, and sparkly baseball caps far too funky for ballet people.

WILLIAM HARPER JEWELRY

Peter Joseph Gallery, 745 Fifth Ave.; (212) 751-5500

In 1995, jewelry designer William Harper created a special one-of-a-kind, ballet-inspired collection to benefit American Ballet Theater. Fashioned from cloisonné enamel, gold, silver, and semiprecious stones, the baubles include "Shove Gives a Push," a necklace inspired by dancer/choreographer Twyla Tharp and six brooches that evoke Serge Diaghilev's Ballets Russes. Pieces start at $12,000.

LA RAY

250 W. 57th St.; (212) 586-9664

This tiny office is stocked with point shoes by German footwear maker Eva. The shoes, pricey at $65 a pair, but exquisitely made, come in European pink satin and have very square toes.

NEW YORK CITY BALLET GIFT SHOPS

Mezzanine level, New York State Theater

With two large tables and several big showcases, this seasonal shop is one of the best ballet shops in town. Surprises turn up on the book table amid the company photographs, out-of-print dance magazines, hard-to-find books and tapes and cassettes from NYCB productions. Besides the predictable (T-shirts, mugs and towels with the NYCB logo), the memorabilia table offers novelties, like lyre-shaped earrings. Autographed toe shoes are a staple as are children's toys, including The Ballet Game (in a pink box, naturally).

THE PERFORMING ARTS SHOP
AT THE METROPOLITAN OPERA HOUSE
Lincoln Center

Though opera memorabilia outnumbers dance two to one, this is a BIG concourse level shop, with a wealth of dance music, videos, and other items, from T-shirts and coffee cups to stuffed animals in tutus. Look for a first-rate collection of tapes and cassettes of ballet music. The shop also stocks what seems like every dance performance ever captured on video, including the terrific new Nonesuch collection of New York City Ballet tapes.

REPETTO
30 Lincoln Plaza 10023; (212) 582-3900

Repetto occupies a choice piece of Lincoln Center turf, even if it's tucked in the back of a building, across from the Lincoln Plaza Cinemas. But with its generous, almost claustrophobic, selection of leotards, tights, and knit legwarmers for adults and children, this New York outpost for France's best known maker of dancewear and shoes is worth the hunt. Leotards can be jazzy and stylish (as leotards go), particularly the velours and shiny knits. Besides Repetto point and soft shoes, the shop carries jazz and character shoes by English shoemaker Gamba.

SANSHA

1733 Broadway; (212) 246-6212

This crowded second-floor shop is stocked floor to ceiling with dance clothes and shoes by Sansha, French-designed dancewear made in China. Sansha's knitwear is colorful, with legwarmers in wide stripes of purples, blues and pinks or blacks, blues and grays. Jazz shoes are also rainbow hued. Point shoes come in satin or canvas with either a square box or a narrower box for thin, tapered feet.

And keep in mind—most troupes, from Feld Ballets/NY
to American Ballet Theater, stock company memorabilia, like
T-shirts with troupe logos, and are pleased to sell them year 'round.
Call the main company number for information.

CHAPTER NINE

Bargains

JUST BECAUSE AN ORCHESTRA SEAT for ballet at the Metropolitan Opera House costs $65 doesn't mean dance in New York is uniformly pricey. Good dance can come cheap, even free. Performances by small companies that rent studio space rarely cost more than $10, and free dance festivals are a summer ritual throughout the city. Amateur folk dance groups serve up gratis performances year 'round at a variety of public spaces (see Chapter Two). There are, in fact, dance bargains galore. The following is a small sampling.

～ FREEBIES ～

DANCING IN THE STREETS
131 Varick St.; (212) 989-6830

A producer of dance in public spaces, Dancing in the Streets attracts such topflight performers, it's often hard to believe the productions are free. But since 1983, this lively organization has staged dozens of inventive programs in New York City—and beyond—featuring, among others, Trisha Brown, Lucinda Childs, Streb/Ringside, Urban Bush Women, Ann Carlson, and David Rousseve. Also look for lesser–known experimental dancers as well as seasoned hoofers; Rat-a-Tap-Tap, a citywide festival of percussive dance several years ago, featured master rhythm tappers Gregory Hines, Savion Glover, and Charles "Honi" Coles. As for venues, expect the unexpected, from Shea Stadium to the Ravine in Prospect Park.

LINCOLN CENTER OUT-OF-DOORS
Lincoln Center; (212) 875-5108

This annual Augustfest, begun in 1970, offers free dance, music, and performances in Damrosch Park and throughout Lincoln Center.

MOVEMENT RESEARCH AT THE JUDSON MEMORIAL CHURCH
55 Washington Square South; (212) 477-6854

Free experimental dance performances Monday nights at 8 p.m. sharp. Reservations necessary. The church also sponsors other free dance programs; call (212) 732-1227.

PROSPECT PARK BOATHOUSE

Prospect Park, Brooklyn; (718) 965-8999

Free outdoor dance performances, spring, summer and fall, in a gorgeous setting near a 19th-century cast steel bridge.

WAVE HILL

675 W. 252nd St., Bronx; (718) 549-3200

This breathtaking outdoor setting, which feels more like the Berkshires than the Bronx, hosts several weeks of contemporary dance each summer, produced by Dancing in the Streets.

∼ $12 AND UNDER ∼

DANCE THEATER WORKSHOP AT BESSIE SHÖNBERG THEATER

All performances $12.

DANSPACE AT ST. MARK'S CHURCH

131 E. 10th St.; (212) 674-8194

All performances $10 or TDF voucher (plus $3 Friday–Saturday)

THE FIELD

161 Avenue of the Americas; (212) 691-6969

The Field, an organization that helps performing artists make art, orchestrates marathon performances called Fielddays—five hour showcases for performers who present works up to 12 minutes long. Venues—and performance dates—are fluid, so it's best to get on the mailing list or subscribe to the newsletter (it's free). Marathons are popular with emerging and experimental performers. Admission is $10 for one day or $15 for an entire weekend of performances. The Field also presents showings of works-in-progress by performers who sign on for ten-week workshop sessions. Fee: $5. All Field presentations are noncurated; performers are selected on a first come, first serve basis.

MOVEMENT RESEARCH OPEN PERFORMANCES
28 Avenue A, 3rd floor (unless otherwise noted); (212) 477-6635
An evening of work-in-progress performances, usually the first Tuesday of the month. The evening includes several performances followed by a discussion of the works by artists and audience. Call in advance. Fee: $3.

PERFORMANCE SPACE 122 (PS 122)
150 First Ave.; (212) 477-5288
Performances cost $12 or less; discounts available.

~ DISCOUNT TICKETS ~

BRYANT PARK MUSIC & DANCE TICKETS BOOTH
60 W. 42nd St.; (212) 382-2323
Discounts on same-day tickets for dance performances. Open Tuesday through Sunday; cash only.

Going Backstage

THE BEST WAY TO GO backstage is to befriend a dancer. If that isn't possible, theater tours are an alternative. Unfortunately, almost none of the theaters that offer dance have guided tours. Your best bet is the hour-long Lincoln Center tour, presented several times a day. Though designed primarily for out-of-towners, the tour takes you several places members of the audience rarely get to go.

At the Metropolitan Opera House, for example, you enter through the stage door, same as the dancers. And, on the day I visited, we viewed the stage from the glassed in director's booth, where the lighting crew and other technicians watch the performance. We weren't so lucky at the New York State Theater, where we gazed down, down, down at the stage from the Fourth Ring. But a rehearsal was in progress, which was entertaining.

Indeed, for New Yorkers, the smart time to take the tour is when ballet companies are in residence in both houses. Your chances of seeing a rehearsal or two are good. And the houses seem more festive when they're up and running than during the dog days of August. Tours leave from the Lincoln Center concourse, lower level, and cost $7.75. Reservations advised: (212) 875-5350.

Index

Adelphi University   149
Aequus Dance Studio   109
Alvin Ailey Amerian Dance
  Center   122, 130
Alvin Ailey American Dance
  Theater   24
Alpha-Omega Theatrical Dance
  Co.   32
American Ballet Theater   25, 94
American Ballroom Theater   68
American Repertory Ballet Co.   86
American Spanish Dance Theater/
  Andrea Del Conte   74, 116
American Tap Dance
  Orchestra   69
Mary Anthony Dance Studio   99
Mary Anthony Dance Theater   32
Fred Astaire Dance Studio   109

Balinese American Fusion
  Dance   33
Balkan Dances   158
BALLET
  Alvin Ailey American Dance Center
    122, 130
  Alvin Ailey American Dance
    Theater   24
  American Ballet Theater   25, 94
  American Repertory Ballet Co.   86
  Ballet Academy East   95, 130
  Ballet for Young Audiences   26
  Ballet Hispanico School of Dance
    116, 131
  Ballet School NY   95, 131
  Ballet Shop, The   168
  Ballet Academy East   130
  Bronx Dance Theater   26, 95, 132
  Capezio   169

BALLET cont.
  Connecticut Ballet   89
  Dance Recordings and Shoes   170
  Dance Theater of Harlem   27
  Danskin   170
  Daring Project, The   28
  Larry Farley   171
  Feld Ballets/NY   28
  Freed of London   171
  Gallery at Lincoln Center,   171
  William Harper Jewelry   172
  Hartford Ballet   89
  Ilya Gaft Dance Theater   29
  Joffrey Ballet School /American
    Ballet Center   96, 135
  La Ray   172
  Manhattan Ballet Company   29
  Manhattan Ballet School, The   96
  Lucy Moses School for Music
    and Dance   96, 136
  Neubert Ballet Institute   97, 136
  New Ballet School, The   136
  New Choreographers on Point/
    Ballet Builders   30
  New Haven Ballet   90
  New Jersey Ballet Company   88
  New York Ballet Institute   97
  New York City Ballet   30
  New York City Ballet Gift Shops
    172
  New York Conservatory of Dance   97
  New York International Ballet
    Competition   166
  New York School of Classical Dance
    98, 137
  New York Theater Ballet   31
  Performing Arts Shop at the
    Metropolitan Opera House,   173

BALLET cont.
  Repetto   173
  Sansha   174
  School of American Ballet   138
  School of Dance Theater of Harlem
    98, 139
  Stamford City Ballet   92
  Staten Island Ballet   32
  Staten Island Ballet School   140

Ballet Academy East   95, 130
Ballet for Young Audiences   26
Ballet Hispanico   74
Ballet Hispanico School of Dance
  116, 131
Ballet School NY   95, 131
Ballet Shop, The   168

BALLROOM DANCE
  Aequus Dance Studio   109
  American Ballroom Theater   68
  Fred Astaire Dance Studios   109
  Ballroom Dancentre   110
  Margaret Batiuchok   110
  Sandra Cameron Dance Center   110
  Club Broadway 2   152
  Kitty Concannon   111
  Copacabana   152
  Dance Manhattan   111
  Dance New York   112
  Dance Recordings and Shoes   170
  Dancesport   112
  Danel & Maria   113
  Eddie Dorfer and Mercedes Colon
    113
  Pierre Dulaine   114
  Fifth Avenue Ballroom   114
  Hideaway   152
  Imperial Society of Teachers
    of Dancing   165

BALLROOM DANCE cont.
  Latin Quarter   152
  Marc Ballroom   153
  Saturday Night Ballroom at the
    92nd Street Y   153
  Polite Society   91
  Tito Puente & Eddie Torres School
    for the Performing Arts   114
  Rainbow Room, The   153
  Roseland   153
  S.O.B.'s   154
  Stepping Out   115
  Strictly Ballroom   115
  Supper Club, The   154
  United States Ballroom
    Championships   165
  Vintage Dance Society   156
  YWCA at 53rd & Lex.   116, 128

Ballroom Dancentre   110
Bard College   148
Barnard College/Columbia Univ.   144
Laban Bartenieff Institute
  of Movement Studies   146
Margaret Batiuchok   110
Nanette Bearden Contemporary
  Dance Theater   33
Robin Becker & Company   34
Lori Belilove & Company   34
Maria Benitez Teatro Flamenco   75
Beverly Blossom   35
Bosilek Bulgarian Folk Dance
  Ensemble   80
Bouwerie Boys Morris Dancers   80
Brant Lake Camp   141
Broadway Dance Center   122, 132
Bronx Dance Theater   26, 95, 132
Brooklyn Academy of Music   14
Brooklyn Center for the Performing
  Arts at Brooklyn College   15

Ron Brown/Evidence   35
Trisha Brown Company   36
Bryant Park Music & Dance Tickets
  Booth   178
Brenda Bufalino/American Tap
  Dance Orchestra   105
Donald Byrd/The Group   36

Sandra Cameron Dance Center   110
CAMPS
  Brant Lake Camp   141
  Chautauqua Dance   141
  Usdan Center for the Creative &
    Performing Arts   142
Pat Cannon   117
Pat Cannon Foot & Fiddle Dance
  Company   75
Capezio   169
Casa Latina   169
Chautauqua Dance   141
Chelsea Piers Roller Rinks   162
Chen & Dancers   37
Nai-Ni Chen Dance Company   87
Lucinda Childs Dance Company   37
Yoshiko Chuma & The School
  of Hard Knocks   38
City Center Theater   15
City College of New York   144
Club Broadway   152
Leon Collins Tap Dance Studio   105
Jane Comfort & Company   38
Kitty Concannon   111
Connecticut Ballet   89
Connecticut College   149
Colin Connor   39
CONTEMPORARY DANCE. See
MODERN AND CONTEMPORARY
Context Studios   18

Copacabana   152
Heather Cornell   106
COUNTRY DANCE. See FOLK AND
COUNTRY DANCE
Country Dance and Song Society   170
Country Dance New York   158
Coyote Dancers   39
Creach/Koester   40
Merce Cunningham Dance Co.   40
Merce Cunnigham Dance Studio
  18, 99

Dance Manhattan   111
Dance New York   112
Dance Notation Bureau   145
Dance Recordings and Shoes   170
Dance Space Inc.   123
Dance Theater of Harlem   27
Dance Theater Workshop at Bessie
  Schönberg Theater   177
Dancebrazil   76
Dances Patrelle   27
Dancesport   112
Dancing in the Streets   176
Danel & Maria   113
Danskin   170
Danspace at St. Mark's Church   177
Daring Project, The   28
Laura Dean Musicians and Dancers   41
Deanna's   156
Denishawn Repertory Dancers/NJ
  Center Dance Collective   86
Dia Center for the Arts   19
Discovery Programs   133
Djoniba Dance & Drum Center
  117, 133
Eddie Dorfer and Mercedes Colon   113
Carolyn Dorfman Dance Co.   87
David Dorfman Dance   41

Pierre Dulaine   114
Duncan Dance Continuum   41
Isadora Duncan Foundation for
  Contemporary Dance   100, 133
Douglas Dunn & Dancers   42

Eiko & Koma   42
Doug Elkins Dance Company   43
ETHNIC DANCE
  American Spanish Dance Theater/
    Andrea Del Conte   74, 116
  Ballet Hispanico   74
  Ballet Hispanico School of Dance
    116, 131
  Maria Benitez Teatro Flamenco   75
  Pat Cannon   117
  Pat Cannon Foot & Fiddle Dance
    Company   75
  Casa Latina   169
  Country Dance and Song Society
    170
  Dance Recordings and Shoes   170
  Dancebrazil   76
  Djoniba Dance and Drum Center
    117, 133
  Fareta School of Dance & Drum
    117, 134
  Flamenco Latino   76
  Donny Golden   76
  Donny Golden School of Irish
    Dance   134
  Japan Society   77
  La Conja Mimbre y Vareta   77
  Lotus Music & Dance   118
  Chas. Moore Dance Theater 124,78
  Liliana Morales   118
  Noche Flamenca   78
  Pilar Rioja   79
  Roots of Brazil   79

ETHNIC DANCE cont.
  Serena Studios   118
  Tachibana Dance Group   84
European Folk Festival   81

Garth Fagan Dance   43
Fareta School of Dance and Drum
  117, 134
Larry Farley   171
Feld Ballets/NY   28
Molissa Fenley   44
Field, The   177
Fifth Avenue Ballroom   114
Flamenco Latino   76
FOLK AND COUNTRY DANCE
  Balkan Dances   158
  Bosilek Bulgarian Folk Dance
    Ensemble   80
  Bouwerie Boys Morris Dancers   80
  Country Dance New York   158
  European Folk Festival   81
  Half Moon Sword   81
  Irish Traditional Dancing   159
  Israeli Folk Dance   159
  Japanese Classical and
    Folk Dancing   160
  Limbora Slovak Folk Ensemble   81
  Louisiana Community Bar
    and Grill   160
  New Scotland Dancers   82
  New World Sword   82
  New York Metropolitan Country
    Music Association   160
  Polish American Folk Dance   83
  Ring O'Bells   83
  Royal Scottish Country Dance
    Society   161
  Scandinavian Couple-Turning
    Dances   161

Swedish Folk Dancers of New York 83, 162

Tomov Folk Dance Ensemble 84

Freed of London 171

Gallery at Lincoln Center, 171

Annabelle Gamson Dance Co. 45

Mimi Garrard Dance Theater 44

Gelabert Studios 120

GhettOriginal 69, 104

Glitter 172

Jane Goldberg 106

Donny Golden 76

Donny Golden School of Irish Dance 134

Mark Goodman 106

David Gordon/Pick Up Co. 45

Martita Goshen's Earthworks 45

Zvi Gotheiner & Dancers 46

Florence Gould Hall 17

Gowanus Arts Exchange 124

Martha Graham Dance Company 46

Martha Graham School of Contemporary Dance 100, 134

Brian Green 104

Chuck Green 107

Half Moon Sword 81

William Harper Jewelry 172

Hartford Ballet 89

Erick Hawkins Dance Company 47

Erick Hawkins School of Dance 100, 135

Hideaway 152

HIP-HOP
  GhettOriginal 69, 104
  Brian Green 104
  Knicks City Dancers 71

HIP-HOP cont.
  Limelight 157
  Mickey D. & Friends 71
  Palladium 157
  Don Philpott 104
  Sound Factory 158

Lisa Hopkins 107

Hunter College, The City University of New York 145

Ice Theater of New York 85

Ilya Gaft Dance Theater 29

Imperial Society of Teachers of Dancing 165

Infinity Dance Theater 48

Irish Traditional Dancing 159

Isadora Duncan Foundation for Contemporary Dance 100, 133

Israeli Folk Dance 159

Andrew Jannetti & Dancers 48

Japan Society 77

Japanese Classical and Folk Dancing 160

Risa Jaroslow & Dancers 49

JAZZ DANCE
  Glitter 172
  Jazz Dance America 70
  Jazzdance by Danny Buraczeski 70
  Knicks City Dancers 71
  Luigi's Jazz Center 103
  Mickey D. & Friends 71
  Radio City Music Hall Rockettes 72
  Silver Belles 72

Jazz Dance America 70

Jazzdance by Danny Buraczeski 70

Joffrey Ballet School/American Ballet Center 96, 135

Bill T. Jones/Arnie Zane Dance Co.   49
Joyce Theater   17
Judson Memorial Church   19
Juilliard School   145

Sylvia & Danny Kaye Playhouse   17
Kitchen Center for Music and Video   19
Susan Klein School of Dance   121
Knicks City Dancers   71

La Conja Mimbre y Vareta   77
La MaMa Experimental Theater
   Club   20
La Place on the Park   157
La Ray   172
Phyllis Lamhut   50
LATIN DANCE
   Club Broadway 2   152
   Copacabana   152
   Hideaway   152
   Latin Quarter   152
Latin Quarter   152
Herve Le Goff   107
Lehman Center for the Performing
   Arts   15
Richard Lemon   50
Lezly Skate School   119
Limbora Slovak Folk Ensemble   81
Limelight   157
Limón Institute   101
Limón Dance Comapny   51
Lincoln Center Out-of-Doors   176
Lotus Music & Dance   118
Louisiana Community Bar
   and Grill   160
Lar Lubovitch Dance Comapny   51
Luigi's Jazz Center   103

Majestic Theater   16
Manhattan Ballet Company   29
Manhattan Ballet School,   96, 135
Manhattan Tap   71
Michael Mao Dance   52
Marc Ballroom   153
Fiona Marcotty Dances   52
Susan Marshall & Company   52
Marymount Manhattan College   146
MEGASTUDIOS
   Alvin Ailey American Dance Center
      122, 130
   Broadway Dance Center   122, 132
   Bronx Dance Theater   26, 95, 132
   Dance Space Inc.   123
   Gowanus Arts Exchange   124
   Charles Moore Dance Studio   124
   New Dance Group Arts Center   124
   92nd Street Y   125
   Perry Dance II   126, 147
   Soundance Studio   102, 140
   Spoke the Hub Dancing   65, 126,
      140
   Steps on Broadway   127, 140
   Times Circle Rehearsal Studios
      127
   West Side Dance Project   128
   YWCA at 53rd and Lexington   116,
      128
Metropolitan Opera House   16
Mickey D. & Friends   71
Midsummer Night Swing   154
Bebe Miller Company   53
Joan Miller's Dance Players   54
MODERN AND CONTEMPORARY
   Alpha-Omega Theatrical Dance
      Company   32
   Mary Anthony Dance Studio   99

MODERN AND CONTEMPORARY

Mary Anthony Dance Theater   32
Balinese American Fusion Dance   33
Nanette Bearden Contemporary
    Dance Theater   33
Robin Becker & Company   34
Lori Belilove & Company   34
Beverly Blossom   35
Ron Brown/Evidence   35
Trisha Brown Company   36
Donald Byrd/The Group   36
Capezio   169
Chen & Dancers   37
Nai-Ni Chen Dance Company   87
Lucinda Childs Dance Company   37
Yoshiko Chuma & The School
    of Hard Knocks   38
Jane Comfort & Company   38
Colin Connor   39
Coyote Dancers   39
Creach/Koester   40
Merce Cunningham Dance Co.   40
Merce Cunningham Studio   18, 99
Danskin   170
Laura Dean Musicians
    and Dancers   41
Denishawn Repertory Dancers/NJ
    Center Dance Collective   86
Carolyn Dorfman Dance Co.   87
David Dorfman Dance   41
Duncan Dance Continuum   41
Isadora Duncan Foundation
    for Contemporary Dance   100, 133
Douglas Dunn & Dancers   42
Eiko & Koma   42
Doug Elkins Dance Company   43
Garth Fagan Dance   43
Molissa Fenley   44
Annabelle Gamson Dance Co.   45

MODERN AND CONTEMPORARY

Mimi Garrard Dance Theater   44
David Gordon/Pick Up Co.   45
Martita Goshen's Earthworks   45
Zvi Gotheiner & Dancers   46
Martha Graham Dance Co.   46
Martha Graham School of
    Contemporary Dance   100, 134
Erick Hawkins Dance Co.   47
Erick Hawkins School of Dance
    100, 135
Infinity Dance Theater   48
Andrew Jannetti & Dancers   48
Risa Jaroslow & Dancers   49
Joffrey Ballet School/American
    Ballet Center   96, 135
Bill T. Jones/Arnie Zane Dance Co.   49
Phyllis Lamhut   50
Richard Lemon   50
Limón Institute   101
Limón Dance Company   51
Lar Lubovitch Dance Company   51
Michael Mao Dance   52
Fiona Marcotty Dances   52
Susan Marshall & Company   52
Bebe Miller Company   53
Joan Miller's Dance Players   54
Momix   90
Elisa Monte Dance   54
Mark Morris Dance Group   55
Movement Research   101
Jennifer Muller/The Works   55
Yves Musard & Vadancers   56
National Dance Institute   136
Neo Labos   56
Phoebe Neville Dance Co.   57
Nikolais and Murray Louis Dance
    Company   57
Nikolias and Louis Dance Lab   102

MODERN AND CONTEMPORARY
92nd Street Y Harkness Dance
Center   137
Tere O'Connor Dance   58
Parsons Dance Company   58
Peridance Ensemble   59
Stephen Petronio Company   59
Pilobolus Dance Theater   91
Eleo Pomare Dance Company   60
Claire Porter   60
Peter Pucci Plus Dancers   61
Dana Reitz   61
Pascal Rioult Dance Theater   61
Nicholas Rodriguez & Dance
Compass   88
David Rousseve/Reality   62
Lynn Shapiro Dance Company   62
Ton Simons and Dancers   63
Anna Sokolow's Player's Project   63
Solomons Company/Dance,   64
Soundance Repertory Co.   64
Soundance Studio   102, 140
Spoke the Hub Dancing   65, 126, 140
Roseanne Spradlin   65
Paul Taylor Dance Company   65
Paul Taylor School   102
Urban Bush Women   66
Doug Varone and Dancers   66
White Oak Dance Project   67
Kevin Wynn Collection   67
Bill Young & Dancers   68

Momix   90
Montclair State University   150
Elisa Monte Dance   54
Charles Moore Dance Studio   124
Charles Moore Dance Theater   78
Lilliana Morales   118
Mark Morris Dance Group   55

Lucy Moses School for Music and
Dance   96, 136
Movement Research   101
Movement Research at the Judson
Memorial Church   176
Movement Research Open
Performances   178
Jennifer Muller/The Works   55
Yves Musard & Vadancers   56

National Dance Institute   136
Neo Labos   56
Neubert Ballet Institute   97, 136
Phoebe Neville Dance Co.   57
New Ballet School   136
New Choreographers on
Point/Ballet Builders   30
New Dance Group Arts Center   124
New Haven Ballet   90
New Jersey Ballet Company   88
New School for Social Research,   146
New Scotland Dancers   82
New World Sword   82
New York Ballet Institute   97
New York City Ballet (NYCB)   30
New York City Ballet Gift Shops   172
New York Conservatory of Dance   97
New York International Ballet
Competition   166
New York Metropolitan Country
Music Association   160
New York School of Classical
Dance   98, 137
New York State Theater   16
New York Swing Dance Society   155
New York Theater Ballet   31
New York University, School
of Education   147

.New York University, Tisch
  School of the Arts   147
Nikolais and Murray Louis Dance
  Company   57
Nikolias and Louis Dance Lab   102
92nd Street Y   125
92nd Street Y Harkness Dance
  Center   137
92nd Street Y, Saturday Night
  Ballroom   153

Noche Flamenca   78
North River Bar   155
NYC Skate Crew   85

Tere O'Connor Dance   58
Ohio Theater   20

Palladium   157
Parsons Dance Company   58
Performance Space 122
  (PS 122)   20, 178
Performing Arts Shop at the
  Metropolitan Opera House,   173
Perichild   138
Peridance Ensemble   59
Perry Dance II   126, 147
Stephen Petronio Company   59
Don Philpott   104
Pilates Studio, The   121
Pilobolus Dance Theater   91
Playhouse 91   18
Polish American Folk Dance   83
Polite Society   91
Max Pollak   108
Eleo Pomare Dance Company   60
Claire Porter   60
Prospect Park Boathouse   177
Peter Pucci Plus Dancers   61

Tito Puente & Eddie Torres
  School for the Performing Arts   114
Purchase College, The State
  University of New York   148

Radio City Music Hall Rockettes   72
Rainbow Room, The   153
Dana Reitz   61
Repetto   173
Ring O'Bells   83
Pilar Rioja   79
Pascal Rioult Dance Theater   61
Nicholas Rodriguez & Dance
  Compass   88
Roller Rinks at Chelsea Piers   118,
  138, 162
Zena Rommett Floor-
  Barre Technique   121
Roots of Brazil   79
Roseland, The   153
David Rousseve/Reality   62
Roxy   162
Royal Scottish Country Dance
  Society   161
Rutgers, The State University
  of New Jersey   150

Sansha   174
Sarah Lawrence College   148
Scandinavian Couple-Turning
  Dances   161
Bessie Schönberg Theater   21
School of American Ballet   138
School of Dance Theater of Harlem
  98, 139
School of the Ice Theater of New
  York   120
Serena Studios   118
Lynn Shapiro Dance Company   62

Silver Belles   72
Ton Simons and Dancers   63
SKATE DANCE
  Ice Theater of New York   85
  Lezly Skate School   119
  NYC Skate Crew   85
  Roller Rinks at Chelsea Piers   119,
    138, 162
  Roxy   162
  School of the Ice Theater
    of New York   120
S.O.B.'s   154
Anna Sokolow's Player's Project   63
Solo Arts Group Inc. (SAGI)   21
Solomons Company/Dance,   64
Sound Factory   158
Soundance Repertory Co.   64
Soundance Studio   102, 140
Peggy Spina Studio   108
Spoke the Hub Dancing   65, 126,
  140
Roseanne Spradlin   65
Squid Dance Performance Space   21
St. Mark's Church In-the-Bowery   20
Stamford City Ballet   92
Staten Island Ballet   32
Staten Island Ballet School   140
Stepping Out   115
Steps on Broadway   127, 140
Strictly Ballroom   115
Supper Club, The   154
Swedish Folk Dancers of New York
  83, 162
SWING DANCE
  Imperial Society of Teachers
    of Dancing   165
  Midsummer Night Swing   154
  New York Swing Dance Society   155

North River Bar   155
United States Ballroom
  Championships   165
Symphony Space   18

Tachibana Dance Group   84
TAP DANCE
  American Tap Dance Orchestra   69
  Brenda Bufalino/American Tap
    Dance Orchestra   105
  Leon Collins Tap Dance Studio   105
  Heather Cornell   106
  Deanna's   156
  Jane Goldberg   106
  Mark Goodman   106
  Chuck Green   107
  Lisa Hopkins   107
  Knicks City Dancers   71
  La Place on the Park   157
  Herve Le Goff   107
  Manhattan Tap   71
  Max Pollak   108
  Radio City Music Hall Rockettes   72
  Silver Belles   72
  Peggy Spina Studio   108
Tap Express   73
Ten Toe Percussion Ensemble/
  Ira Bernstein   73
Robin Tribble   108
Paul Taylor Dance Company   65
Paul Taylor School   102
Theater at Riverside Church   22
THERAPUTIC DANCE
  Gelabert Studios   120
  Susan Klein School of Dance   121
  Pilates Studio, The   121
  Zena Rommett Floor-
    Barre Technique   121

Times Circle Rehearsal Studios   127
Tomov Folk Dance Ensemble   84
Robin Tribble   108
Trinity College   150

United States Ballroom
  Championships   165
Urban Bush Women   66
Usdan Center for the Creative &
  Performing Arts   142

Doug Varone and Dancers   66
Vintage Dance Society   156

Wave Hill   177
Wesleyan University   150
West Side Dance Project   128
White Oak Dance Project   67
Kevin Wynn Collection   67

Bill Young & Dancers   68
YWCA at 53rd & Lexington   116, 128

∼ ABOUT THE AUTHOR ∼

TERRY TRUCCO took her first ballet lesson at the age of three and has been a dance enthusiast ever since. Besides taking ballet and hip-hop classes, she frequents dance performances, everything from New York City Ballet and experimental companies at St. Mark's Church to visiting Eastern European folk dance troupes. A contributing editor to *Dance Magazine*, she has written about dance for *The New York Times* and many national publications.

∼ ABOUT THE ILLUSTRATOR ∼

EMILY LISKER, whose illustrations have appeared in magazines and newspapers across the country, is currently working on her fourth children's book. She lives in Woonsocket, Rhode Island.